JOHN ELD

ALL
THINGS
NEW

HEAVEN, EARTH,
AND THE RESTORATION OF
EVERYTHING YOU LOVE

STUDY GUIDE | FIVE SESSIONS

NELSON
BOOKS

An Imprint of Thomas Nelson

RANSOMED HEART
LOVE GOD. LIVE FREE.

RANSOMEDHEART.COM

Published in Nashville, Tennessee, by Nelson Books, an imprint of Thomas Nelson. Nelson Books and Thomas Nelson are registered trademarks of HarperCollins Christian Publishing, Inc.

Published in association with Yates & Yates, www.yates2.com.

Unless otherwise indicated, all Scripture quotations are taken from The Holy Bible, New International Version®, NIV®. Copyright © 1973, 1978, 1984, 2011 by Biblica, Inc.® Used by permission. All rights reserved worldwide.

Scripture quotations marked KJV are taken from the King James Version. Public domain.

Scripture quotations marked MSG are taken from *The Message* by Eugene H. Peterson. © 1993, 1994, 1995, 1996, 2000. Used by permission of NavPress Publishing Group. All rights reserved.

Scripture quotations marked NASB are taken from the New American Standard Bible. Copyright © 1960, 1962, 1963, 1968, 1971, 1972, 1973, 1975, 1977, 1995 by The Lockman Foundation. Used by permission (www.Lockman.org).

Scripture quotations marked NKJV are taken from the New King James Version. Copyright © 1982 by Thomas Nelson, a registered trademark of HarperCollins Christian Publishing, Inc. All rights reserved. Used by permission.

Scripture quotations marked NLT are taken from the Holy Bible, New Living Translation. Copyright © 1996, 2004, 2007, 2013, 2015 by Tyndale House Foundation. Used by permission of Tyndale House Publishers, Inc., Carol Stream, Illinois 60188. All rights reserved.

Scripture quotations marked RSV are taken from the Revised Standard Version of the Bible. Copyright © 1946, 1952, and 1971 by the National Council of the Churches of Christ in the United States of America. Used by permission. All rights reserved.

Thomas Nelson titles may be purchased in bulk for educational, business, fund-raising, or sales promotional use. For information, please e-mail SpecialMarkets@ThomasNelson.com.

ISBN 978-0-310-68216-5

First Printing September 2017 / Printed in the United States of America

CONTENTS

INTRODUCTION

Though we are trying to put a bold face on things, the human race is not doing well at all.

We appear to be suffering a great crisis of hope. It's taking place loudly in politics and economies; it's taking place quietly in the hearts of millions at this moment.

When you consider the pain, suffering, and heartbreak contained in one children's hospital, one refugee camp, one abusive home or war-torn village over the course of a single day, it's almost too much to bear. But then consider that multiplied out across the planet, over all the days in a year, then down through history. It would take a pretty wild, astonishing, and breathtaking hope to overcome the agony and trauma of this world.

How is God going to make it all right? How is he going to redeem all the suffering and loss of this world . . . and in your own life?

Escapism isn't going to do it, no matter what religious version you choose. What about all your hopes and dreams? What about all your special places and memories, the things most dear to your heart? Is there no hope for any of that? What we ache for is redemption. What our heart cries out for is *restoration*.

And I have some stunning, breathtaking news for you: *restoration is exactly what Jesus promised*. Despite what you may have been told, he didn't focus your hopes on the great airlift to heaven. He promised "the renewal of all things," including the earth you love, every precious part of it, and your own story (Matthew 19:28). The climax of the entire Bible takes place with these words: "I am making everything new!" (Revelation 21:5). A day of Great Restoration is coming. Not annihilation—*restoration*. That is the only hope powerful enough to be for us what God calls "the anchor for the soul" (Hebrews 6:19).

This study guide is a companion to go along with the book *All Things New* and the five sessions you'll be watching in the video series. (You'll want to have a copy of the book and the video. If you are leading a group, a leader's guide has been provided for you in the back of this study.) I have combined two chapters of the book into each session in this guide, making this a five-part study. So, you will be covering two chapters in the book each time you do the videos or use this study.

Each session in this guide will have three parts:

1. **Personal Preparation:** Before your group meets (I'm assuming you are doing this in a group—though you could also do this study on your own), you'll want to read the corresponding chapters in the book and answer a few questions in this guide.

2. **Group Discussion:** Watch the session video as a group, take some notes, and then talk about it. In this section, I've suggested a few questions to help guide your group's conversation time. (Again, if you are a leader, there's more guidance for you in the leader's guide at the back of the study.)

3. **Group Exercise:** Each week, I provide a "group project" to help stimulate discussion around the concepts you've learned during the session.

I'll be frank: if everything is going wonderfully for you right now, and you have every reason to believe it's going to stay that way, this study probably isn't for you. But if you are wondering why your soul feels so unsettled and what there really is to look forward to, and if you are longing for a wild, astonishing hope that could be an anchor for your life, read on. You're going to be very glad you did.

John

THE HOPE
OF
RENEWAL

Picture a treasure chest.

Not a small box that might hold jewelry on a girl's night-stand—a large treasure chest, larger than any suitcase you own, larger than any suitcase you've ever seen.

Picture a massive oak treasure chest, like pirates might have used, with large iron hinges and a huge clasp. The size and age and strength of this strongbox say it was made for the most valuable things.

Inside this chest are all of the things you wish could somehow be restored to you. Everything you have lost, everything you know you will lose.

What fills your treasure chest?

—JOHN ELDREDGE, *All Things New*

PERSONAL PREPARATION

This week, read chapters 1 and 2 in *All Things New*: "Is There a Hope That Really Overcomes All This?" and "The Renewal of All Things." Let's begin simply and honestly with your reaction to these first two chapters. Our first reaction is often a telling one, revealing places and assumptions in us God wants to speak to. So, without any pressure to get the "answer right," what did this stir in you?

Before we dive into the first chapter, perhaps it will be helpful to give voice to the beliefs, thoughts, and emotions you have surrounding the topic of heaven.

» In a few sentences, write down how you would explain heaven to a neighbor unfamiliar with Scripture. Include your thoughts on what heaven is, where it is, who will be there, and what we will do there.

» How has the New Earth factored into your understanding of heaven?

» Are these beliefs and understandings enough to fuel a deep longing in you for what is to come? If not, what would you say is lacking?

» What questions do you have about heaven and the New Earth?

Is There a Hope That Really Overcomes All This?

Can we just be honest? Life is brutal.

There is just enough goodness to rouse our hearts with expectation, and plenty enough sadness to cut us back down. When the cutting down exceeds the rising up, you wonder if you shouldn't just stay down. "I wept when I was borne," wrote the Anglican poet George Herbert, "and every day shewes why."[1] Yes, life can also be beautiful. I am a lover of all the beautiful things in life. But may I point out that the movie by that name—*Life Is Beautiful*—takes place in a Nazi concentration camp. The story is precious in the way the father loves and protects his little boy from the ghoulish realities all around. But the father is killed at the end. Many, many people die horrible deaths at the end.

We need more than a silver-lining outlook on life. Much, much more. We need an unbreakable, unquenchable hope (*All Things New*, pages 3–4).

» What is an example of a situation where you are currently losing hope?

» What is the hardest aspect of holding on to hope in every situation?

Looking for a Stronger Hope

Scripture names hope as one of the Three Great Forces of human existence:

> Three things will last forever—faith, hope, and love
> (1 Corinthians 13:13 NLT).

By saying they last forever, God names these three as immortal powers. A life without faith has no meaning; a life without love isn't worth living; a life without hope is a dark cavern from which you cannot escape. These things aren't simply "virtues." Faith, hope, and love are mighty *forces* meant to carry your life forward, upward; they are your wings and the strength to use them.

I believe hope plays the critical role. You'll find it pretty hard to love when you've lost hope; hopelessness collapses into *who cares?* And what does it matter that we have faith if we have no hope? Faith is just a rigid doctrine with nothing to look forward to. Hope is the wind in your sails, the spring in your step. Hope is so essential to your being that Scripture calls it "an anchor for the soul" (Hebrews 6:19).

In an untethered world, we need a hope that can anchor us (page 8).

» It might be helpful here to pause and ask a few questions. What would you say is the great hope of your life these days?

» How do you see the mighty forces of faith, hope, and love (see 1 Corinthians 13:13) working together?

» Do you agree that hope plays the critical role? Why or why not?

Eden Restored

Jesus Christ gave his life to give each of us a hope above and beyond all former hopes. Every action and teaching of his brilliant life were very intentionally directed at unveiling this hope to us. Late in the Gospel of Matthew he described it with breathtaking clarity:

> "Truly I tell you, at the renewal of all things, when the Son of Man sits on his glorious throne . . . everyone who has left houses or brothers or sisters or father or mother or wife or children or fields for my sake will receive a hundred times as much and will inherit eternal life" (19:28–29).

At the renewal of all things?! God's intention for us is *the renewal of all things*? This is what the Son of God said; that is how he plainly described it. I can hardly speak. *Really?*

The Greek word used here for "renewal" is *palingenesia*, which is derived from two root words: *paling*, meaning "again," and *genesia*, meaning "beginning," which of course hearkens back to Genesis. Genesis again. Eden restored. Could it possibly be (pages 12–13)?

» In this passage from Matthew, what do you think Jesus means when he says those who have left houses or relatives or fields for his sake will "receive a hundred times as much"? Describe what a hundred-fold increase in each of these three categories might look like.

» Have you ever heard of the Greek word *palingenesia* before? How does the definition of that word—"Genesis again"—change your interpretation of what Jesus meant by the phrase "the renewal of all things"?

The thing you are made for is the renewal of all things. God has given you a heart for his kingdom—not the wispy vagaries of a cloudy heaven, but the sharp reality of the world made new. This is one of the most important things you can know about yourself. Did you know this about yourself? When was the last time you told yourself, as you looked in the mirror in the morning, *Good morning; you have a heart for the kingdom*. This explains so much; it will be such an enormous help to you. It explains your anger and all of your addictions. It explains your cry for justice, and it also explains the growing hopelessness, resignation, cynicism, and defeat.

If we will listen with kindness and compassion to our own souls, we will hear the echoes of a hope so precious we can barely put words to it, a wild hope we can hardly bear to embrace. God put it there. He also breathed the corresponding promise into the earth; it is the whisper that keeps coming to us in moments of golden goodness. But of course. "God has made everything beautiful for its own time. He has planted eternity in the human heart" (Ecclesiastes 3:11 NLT). The secret to your unhappiness and the answer to the agony of the earth are one and the same—we are longing for the kingdom of God. We are aching for the restoration of all things.

That is the only hope strong enough, brilliant enough, glorious enough to overcome the heartache of this world (pages 16–17).

» God has "planted eternity in the human heart." This is one of the most important things you can know about yourself, because it explains your anger, addictions, longing for justice, and so much more. Is this a new thought for you? How does seeing your heart in this way help you navigate the world?

» What are some specific ways that your heart aches for the restoration of all things?

The Renewal of All Things

When Jesus used the phrase "at the renewal of all things," he did it casually, almost breezily. You get the impression he assumed his listeners didn't need an explanation or a long defense of the idea. Jesus spoke as though he were simply drawing upon a story and theology his disciples would know quite well. And indeed, these earnest Jews would have immediately found connection with many Old Testament passages stored in their hearts:

Those the LORD has rescued will return.
They will enter Zion with singing;
everlasting joy will crown their heads.

Gladness and joy will overtake them,
   and sorrow and sighing will flee away (Isaiah 51:11).

"Then you will look and be radiant,
   your heart will throb and swell with joy;
the wealth on the seas will be brought to you,
   to you the riches of the nations will come. . . .

"I will make peace your governor
   and well-being your ruler.
No longer will violence be heard in your land,
   nor ruin or destruction within your borders,
but you will call your walls Salvation
   and your gates Praise.
The sun will no more be your light by day,
   nor will the brightness of the moon shine on you,
for the LORD will be your everlasting light,
   and your God will be your glory.
Your sun will never set again,
   and your moon will wane no more;
the LORD will be your everlasting light,
   and your days of sorrow will end" (Isaiah 60:5, 17–20). . . .

"See, I will create
   new heavens and a new earth.
The former things will not be remembered,
   nor will they come to mind.
But be glad and rejoice forever
   in what I will create,
for I will create Jerusalem to be a delight
   and its people a joy.
I will rejoice over Jerusalem
   and take delight in my people;
the sound of weeping and of crying
   will be heard in it no more" (65:17–19) (pages 21–23).

» What phrase or verse from the above passages in Isaiah resonates most with you? Why?

» Imagine what it will be like when there is no more weeping and crying (see Isaiah 65:19). What does this promise hold for your life?

» What does this promise mean within your circle of friends? In relation to current world events?

Jesus knew his listeners already embraced this hope; he knew they ached for it and prayed for it. This is the culmination of all the Old Testament promises of a Great Restoration. And of course this passage foreshadows the climax of the book of Revelation, where the entire biblical canon swells to a crescendo like a symphony reaching its glorious finish. Here is the final word of God on his promise to us:

Then I saw "a new heaven and a new earth," for the first heaven and the first earth had passed away, and there was no longer any sea. I saw the Holy City, the new Jerusalem, coming down out of heaven from God, prepared as a bride beautifully dressed for her husband. And I heard a loud voice from the throne saying, "Look! God's dwelling place is now among the people, and he will dwell with them. They will be his

people, and God himself will be with them and be
their God. 'He will wipe every tear from their eyes.
There will be no more death' or mourning or crying
or pain, for the old order of things has passed away."

He who was seated on the throne said, "I am
making everything new!" Then he said, "Write this
down, for these words are trustworthy and true"
(21:1–5). . . . .

No matter what translation you prefer, the truth of Revelation 21:5 is quite clear:

"Behold, I make all things new" (KJV, NKJV, RSV).

"Behold, I am making all things new" (NASB).

"Look, I am making everything new" (NLT)!

"Look! I'm making everything new" (MSG) (pages 23–
24, 26).

» What do these passages say about the New Jerusalem and the
renewed earth?

» God states that he will make "all things new" rather than "all new
things." Why is that good news?

Redemption, Not Destruction

Many people have the vague but ominous idea that God destroys the current reality and creates a new "heavenly" one. But that is not what Scripture actually says.

> For all creation is waiting eagerly for that future day when God will reveal who his children really are. Against its will, all creation was subjected to God's curse. But with eager hope, the creation looks forward to the day when it will join God's children in glorious freedom from death and decay. For we know that all creation has been groaning as in the pains of childbirth right up to the present time. And we believers also groan, even though we have the Holy Spirit within us as a foretaste of future glory, for we long for our bodies to be released from sin and suffering. We, too, wait with eager hope for the day when God will give us our full rights as his adopted children, including the new bodies he has promised us (Romans 8:19–23 NLT).

Paul teaches us that creation—meaning the earth and the animal kingdom—longs for the day of its redemption, when "it will join God's children in glorious freedom from death and decay" (verse 21). Clearly that does not imply destruction; far from it. Paul anticipated a joyful day when creation shares in the eternity of the children of God:

> The created world itself can hardly wait for what's coming next. Everything in creation is being more or less held back. God reins it in until both creation and all the creatures are ready and can be released at the same moment into the glorious times ahead (Romans 8:19–21 MSG).

The glorious times ahead, when all things are made new
(pages 26–27).

» What does the promise of the above passage stir in you when
Paul references the "glorious freedom" from death and decay in
our new bodies?

» Annihilation is not nearly as impressive as *redemption*. What does
the promise of a redeemed earth do for your heart?

I know, I know—it's a lot to take in. This is a total reframing for
most of us, even though it has been right there in the Scriptures for centuries. Take a moment; take a deep breath. Get
a glass of water if you need to, or something stronger. You've
just been told your future is "the restoration of all things," real
things, the restoration of everything *you* love.

No wonder it begins with a glorious feast of celebration!
"Blessed are those who are invited to the wedding supper of the
Lamb!" (Revelation 19:9). This wedding reception is also fore-
shadowed in the Jewish expectation of the coming kingdom:

On this mountain the LORD Almighty will prepare
a feast of rich food for all peoples,
a banquet of aged wine—

the best of meats and the finest of wines.
On this mountain he will destroy
   the shroud that enfolds all peoples,
the sheet that covers all nations;
   he will swallow up death forever.
The Sovereign LORD will wipe away the tears
   from all faces;
he will remove his people's disgrace
   from all the earth (Isaiah 25:6–8). . . .

There is a wonderful, tangible depiction of this feast in the book and film *The Fellowship of the Ring*. Bilbo Baggins is celebrating his 111th birthday with an extravagant celebration he throws at his own generous expense. It takes place on a late-summer evening; the countryside is in full bloom. Lanterns are hanging in the trees. Fireworks are going off over an outdoor party—picnic tables, a dance floor, pavilion, live music, laughter, celebration. An entire community is having the time of their lives. When our eldest son, Sam, was getting married and planning the reception, he said, "I want Bilbo's party." Don't you? The joy, ease, companionship, the lightheartedness of it; there is no clock ticking, no curfew, nobody's going to call the police—it just gets to go on and on.

Jesus is personally looking forward to this celebration immensely: "Truly I tell you, I will not drink again from the fruit of the vine until that day when I drink it new in the kingdom of God" (Mark 14:25). Jesus assumes a day is coming when very real things like drinking wine together will take place in the kingdom of God. When all things are made new (pages 31–33).

» It's true. Your future is the restoration of all things. Not just *some* things, but *all* things. What would you love to see restored but feel it is just too much to ask? Invite God into this specific desire now.

» Have you considered how much Jesus is looking forward to the coming Wedding Feast? Does his passion for this gathering increase your anticipation for what this time will be like? Explain.

What Does Restoration Look Like?

Jesus Christ is the forerunner for the Great Renewal, "the beginning and the firstborn from among the dead" (Colossians 1:18). He died, as everyone has and will. But on the third day he was raised to life, leaving his grave clothes folded neatly in the tomb. (A very touching detail, I might add, as if to say, "And that's that," like a man putting away his flannel pajamas now that winter is past.) On Easter morning Jesus walked out of the grave radiantly alive, restored, and everyone recognized him. The "new" Jesus is not someone or something else now; he is the Jesus they loved and knew. He walked with them, had meals with them—just like before. The most striking thing about the post-resurrection activities of Jesus is that they were so remarkably *ordinary*:

Early in the morning, Jesus stood on the shore, but the disciples did not realize that it was Jesus.

He called out to them, "Friends, haven't you any fish?"

"No," they answered.

He said, "Throw your net on the right side of the boat and you will find some." When they did, they were unable to haul the net in because of the large number of fish. . . .

When they landed, they saw a fire of burning coals there with fish on it, and some bread.

Jesus said to them, "Bring some of the fish you have just caught." So Simon Peter climbed back into the boat and dragged the net ashore. It was full of large fish, 153, but even with so many the net was not torn. Jesus said to them, "Come and have breakfast." None of the disciples dared ask him, "Who are you?" They knew it was the Lord. Jesus came, took the bread and gave it to them, and did the same with the fish (John 21:4–6, 9–13).

This is such a homely scene, so commonplace, the sort of thing you'd expect to run into along the shore of Lake Michigan or the Mississippi. Just a group of guys hanging out at the beach, cooking breakfast for some friends. Jesus' restored life is surprisingly like his "former" life. As will be drinking wine at the feast; as will be the feast itself (how many of you realize you eat in the life to come?!) (pages 33–35).

» John references that Jesus is not someone or something else after his resurrection but the same Jesus his disciples loved and knew. Does this insight bring more clarity to what your restored body and life might look like in the coming kingdom?

» Have you considered that we will eat and drink in the life to come? What do you imagine the food and drink will taste like in the coming kingdom?

The Great Renewal rescues us from all the vague, ethereal, unimaginable visions we've been given of an eternal life Somewhere Up Above. When Jesus speaks of the Restoration, he does so in very tangible terms, pointing to the recovery of normal things like houses and lands:

> "Truly I tell you, at the renewal of all things, when the Son of Man sits on his glorious throne . . . everyone who has left houses or brothers or sisters or father or mother or wife or children or fields for my sake will receive a hundred times as much and will inherit eternal life" (Matthew 19:28–29).

There is no bait and switch here. The renewal of all things simply means that the earth you love—all your special places and treasured memories—is restored and renewed and given back to you. Forever. Nobody seems to have heard this or paid much attention to it because, for one thing, nobody I know is fantasizing about it. When was the last time you eavesdropped on a conversation at Starbucks about the restoration of all things? And for another thing, everybody I talk to still has these anemic, wispy views of heaven, as a place up there somewhere, where we go to attend the eternal-worship-service-in-the-sky.

Meanwhile we fantasize about that boat we'd love to get or the trip to Italy, the chocolate éclair or the girl in the cubicle next door. Of course we do—we are made for utter happiness.

But the restoration of all things—now that would change everything (pages 35–36).

» What does the promise that all your special places and treasured memories will be restored and renewed stir in you?

» List specific places you most look forward to seeing afresh in the New Earth. Explain why.

We have quite a stunning present to unpack, dear readers, and future sessions to do it some justice. But we must prepare our hearts to receive such a gift, or it will wash over us like rain on hard ground.

THE BIG IDEAS

» We need an unbreakable, unquenchable hope.
» Jesus gave his life to provide a hope above and beyond all former hopes—the renewal of all things (see Matthew 19:28–29).
» Annihilation is not nearly as impressive as redemption. God chooses to redeem rather than destroy this earth.

GROUP DISCUSSION

Watch the video for session 1. If you find it helpful, use the following space to take a few notes on anything that stood out to you.

Teaching Notes

Discussion Questions

After the teaching session has ended, discuss as a group any or all of the following questions.

1. **Read Hebrews 6:19.** It is essential for you to have an unbreakable, unquenchable hope as the anchor of your soul. If your life has this anchor, how does it affect the way you react to hardships? If you are missing this anchor and feel adrift, can you name when you first lost the hope and confident anticipation that goodness was coming?

2. How you envision your future impacts your current experience more than anything else. If you knew God was going to restore your life and everything you love any day—not in a vague heaven but right here on this earth—what would that do for you?

3. **Read Matthew 19:28–29.** The word "renewal" comes from the Greek word *palingenesia*. It is derived from two root words: *palin*, meaning "again," and *genesia*, meaning "beginning." How does seeing the New Earth as "Eden restored" expand your anticipation of what awaits us?

4. The Greek word *apocatastasis* can be defined as "to put something back into its original condition; to restore something to its created glory." How does this help your understanding of the way God plans to restore everything . . . including you?

5. For too long, Christians have misunderstood their destiny. We have thought we would leave the earth we love and go to an ethereal "heaven" somewhere as the earth was destroyed. Was this your view? If so, how did it make you feel?

6. **Read Revelation 19:9.** What are you most looking forward to at the actual Wedding Feast of the Lamb? Who would you

love to sit by? What would you say as you raise your glass and offer a toast?

7. In this first session, what stood out to you as the most surprising or new revelation about heaven, the New Earth, or the coming restoration? How would embracing this view change the way you face each day?

GROUP EXERCISE

As a group, close your eyes and spend several minutes thinking about the treasure chest described on first page of this session. Inside are all things that will be restored to you—the things you have lost or will lose. After a few minutes, share with one another the contents of your treasure chest.

CREATION MADE NEW

I dreamed of the kingdom last night.

This time I saw horses, fifty or sixty at least, galloping through fields of tall grasses. . . . The grace and freedom of their thundering stride was captivating. I thought perhaps they were wild horses; then I saw riders among them.

Suddenly I, too, was among them, riding with them. We came to an embankment and stream crossing. Horse and rider amended their gait, and soon as we were over, took off again like the wind. It was a glorious game of sorts, a romp.

When I woke I thought, *Surely I am making this up*. I had breakfast and drove to work. There, on a city corner, where I have never seen such a sight in twenty years of living here, were riders on horseback. As if Jesus were saying, *Now do you believe me?*

Yes. I do.

—JOHN ELDREDGE, *All Things New*

PERSONAL PREPARATION

This week, read chapters 3 and 4 in *All Things New*: "Let Us Be Honest" and "The New Earth." Let's begin again simply with your reaction to the chapters. What did this stir in you?

Let Us Be Honest

Like our shadow, the truth is always there; we don't often look at it, but we know—life is a long series of good-byes. You've already said good-bye to your childhood years, and with them probably your hometown and the house you were raised in, not to mention your childhood friends. The best of us might hang on to one or two playmates from our youth, but catching pollywogs with Danny down in the creek just isn't recovered through a Christmas card. If you had a beloved childhood pet, you have said that hard good-bye as well; I've had clients for whom it remained one of their life's greatest wounds. Most of us said farewell to first sweethearts, feeling as though some golden part of our innocence was left behind with them. Most of you have left your first apartment after being married and all the sweet memories there.

If you stop and think about it, you've said a lot of good-byes in your life so far. And fight it as we may, we know down deep that many more are coming. I think that's why I hate even small good-byes, like when the kids leave after a Thanksgiving visit. Stasi said to me last time, "This is our life now—saying good-bye."

Oh, friends—this is why hope is so very precious. It is our lifeline, the anchor of our souls. And this is why it is so important to know where our hope is, to help it land in the right places (*All Things New*, pages 43–44).

» Do you agree with the statement that life is a long series of good-byes? Why or why not?

» How do you handle good-byes this side of the kingdom? How do you look to hope as the anchor of your soul in this season?

Protecting Hope

When our hopes are in their proper places, attached to the right things, not only do we flourish better as human beings, but we are rescued from a thousand heartbreaks. For not all hopes are created equal; there are casual hopes, precious hopes, and ultimate hopes.

Casual hopes are the daily variety: "I sure hope it doesn't rain this weekend"; "I hope we can get tickets to the game"; "I really hope this flight is on time." Nothing wrong with this brand of hope; it is human nature to have it. I think it is the sign of a healthy soul when we often use the words "I hope." My wife does. "I hope this pie turns out," meaning she cares about the dinner she is hosting. "I hope we get to the Tetons next year," meaning she cares about dreams and family memories. Hope shows your heart is still alive.

But of course, those casual hopes are nothing when compared to our precious hopes: "I hope this pregnancy goes well"; "I hope God hears my prayers for Sally"; "I hope the CT scan turns out to reveal nothing at all." Precious hopes are far deeper to our hearts, and they tend to fuel our most earnest prayers.

Deeper still lie our ultimate hopes, our life-and-death hopes. I would suggest that the only things that belong in the category of ultimate hopes are the things that will destroy your heart and soul if they are not fulfilled. "I hope God can forgive me." "I hope somehow my mistakes can be redeemed." "I hope I will see you again" (pages 45–46).

» What are three of your *casual* hopes?

1.
2.
3.

» What are three current *precious* hopes?

1.
2.
3.

» Finally, what are three of your *ultimate* hopes?

1.
2.
3.

You'll notice that many people have let their hopes go wandering—they have made casual hopes into precious hopes and turned genuinely precious hopes into critical or ultimate hopes. The person who commits suicide because their loved one chose another has taken a precious hope and made it the outcome of their very being.

I would say that when a casual hope is deferred, we are disappointed but no more. We are downcast for a moment or a day. When a precious hope is dashed, it can really break your heart. You may not recover for a week or five years, depending on the loss and the other resources of your life. "Hope deferred makes the heart sick" (Proverbs 13:12). Doesn't it, though?

But when an *ultimate* hope goes unanswered, the result is devastation from which you will never recover. . . .

Here is my point: the renewal of all things is meant to be your first hope in the way that God is your First Love. If it isn't the answer to your wildest dreams, if you aren't ready at this very moment to sell everything and buy this field, then you have placed your hopes somewhere else.

Nearly everyone has (pages 46–47).

» It's easy to let our hopes go wandering. What is a recent example of where you've turned a casual hope into a precious or even ultimate hope?

» Is the renewal of all things your first and greatest hope? If not, can you name what you have placed your hope in?

Looking for the Kingdom

"What's on your bucket list?" is standard cocktail party fare and a question used in interviews when the potential employer is trying to "get to know you."

I've had an embarrassing reaction to bucket lists for some time, and only recently have I understood why. Friends and acquaintances will speak excitedly about something on their bucket list—sailing to Tahiti, visiting the Holy Land, taking a motorcycle trek through Asia—and I feel completely baffled. At first I thought it was because I don't have a bucket list, can't even name the top things that would make my list, and I thought, *Maybe I don't allow myself to dream.* But clarity came as I thought more about the Restoration.

The renewal of all things is meant to be the center of our view of the world, our hopes, and our tangible expectations as we plan our lives going forward. The phrase *bucket list* comes from the expression "kick the bucket," the day we give it all up. A bucket list means those things we hope to do before we die. Meaning, it's now or never, baby. Bucket list mentality is very revealing and even more tragic, because it betrays our belief that this life *really* is our only chance. After all—we think the earth is destroyed and we go to the pews in the sky. No wonder the human race grows more desperate in our search for kingdom counterfeits (page 50).

» You have a heart for the kingdom, for the Great Restoration. What are you presently doing with it? What are you fantasizing about? Where we take our fantasies is a helpful way to know what we are doing with our kingdom heart.

» How does this section reframe your thoughts on the need for a "bucket list"?

Facing the Inevitable

You will say the last good-bye to your parents. It is inevitable. God forbid you have to say the last good-bye to your child.

What is it, my readers, that you hope to hang on to? If you love your athletic condition, surely you realize it cannot go on forever; eventually your body will succumb to age and your performance will diminish every year. Inexorably. If you relish your mind, you understand that your mind will dim with age; even if you dodge the great leveler dementia, you will forget many things, and may eventually have the mental capacity of a small child. And the people you love? You will lose them or they you; your very life is but a passing breeze, "each of us is but a breath" (Psalm 39:5 NLT). The fall and winter of your life will come; they are perhaps upon many of you even now. There is no holding back that winter.

You understand, dear friends, that you will say good-bye to everyone you love and everything you hold dear. . . .

There is only the kingdom, friends. Everything else will slip through your fingers, no matter how strong your grasp. Why do we fight this hope, keeping it at arm's length? We nod in appreciation but ask it to stay outside our yard. . . .

But when you raise the white flag, when you finally accept the truth that you will lose everything one way or another, utterly, irrevocably—then the Restoration is news beyond your wildest dreams (pages 52, 56–57).

» What do you hang your hopes on? Is it hard to accept that ultimately it too will fade?

» When we finally raise the white flag and accept the truth that we will lose everything one way or another, the Restoration becomes news beyond our wildest dreams. Have you raised the white flag yet? If so, what did it take for you to get to that point? If not, what is causing you to wait?

What If?

As we sat in the bleachers, unable to stop the unfolding ceremony, watching our youngest son Luke slowly approach the stage in cap and gown, I was on the brink of sobbing shamelessly. *How is this not just loss?* my heart cried to God. *Tell me—how is everything not just loss?* At that moment everything felt like loss.

Jesus replied immediately, *Oh, John—nothing is lost.*

Some of you may have experienced in a sermon or during personal Bible study, perhaps in a time of prayer or in a counselor's office, the ability of Jesus to communicate an entire concept in a single moment. You have a revelation. The Creator of our mind and soul can give to us a sweeping understanding as if by transfusion. If I put into words the revelation given in that moment in the forty-second row at an ordinary high school commencement, Jesus showed me something like this:

> When the kingdom comes, my dear, heartbroken friend, nothing that was precious to you in this life will be lost. No memory, no event, none of your story or theirs, nothing is lost. How could it be lost? It is all held safe in the heart of the infinite God, who encompasses all things. Held safe outside of time in the treasuries of the kingdom, which transcends yet honors all time. This will all be given back to you at the Restoration, just as surely as your sons will come back to you. Nothing is lost.

The effect was nearly instantaneous. I went from a desolate parent saying good-bye—not just to our last child but to an entire era—to a beloved son who had just been given a sneak preview of the Christmas morning that will come upon all the earth. I underwent a complete emotional transformation. All time had stopped in the moment before that moment; now I was completely fine. My body relaxed back into the chair like a man who had just set forth on a Caribbean cruise. I wanted to shout out, "You can carry on—I'm good now."

Nothing is lost.

If you will just let go of your anger and cynicism for a moment, just allow it to be true for a moment, well then—your heart is going to take a pretty deep breath (pages 57–59).

» Describe when you recently mourned the loss of a season or a person. In that moment—where everything felt like loss—how were you able to sense God's presence?

» Do you struggle with the promise that nothing will be lost? If so, what is the hardest aspect of it for you to embrace or believe?

The New Earth

We are preparing our hearts to receive the hope that alone can be the anchor of our souls. One day soon you will step into a renewed earth, a young earth, sparkling like an orchard of cherry trees after a rain shower. Joy will be yours. How do we open our hearts to this after so much pain and disappointment? We have lost many things as we've passed through the battlefields of this war-torn world; our humanity has been stripped of such essential goodness. One of our greatest losses is the gift of wonder, the doorway into the kingdom heart. But each of us has special places and favorite stories that are still able to reawaken it. . . .

Narnia, Middle Earth, Pandora, Tatooine—they are all new worlds and yet not *entirely* new. There are trees and streams, deserts and animals like enough to our own world to be familiar, yet different enough to be enchanting. Chesterton believed this was the secret to romance—the blend of the familiar and new, "to be at once astonished at the world and yet at home in it."[2] He felt the reason every age still reads fairy tales is actually not to escape our world but to *re-enchant* it: "These tales say that apples were golden only to refresh the forgotten moment when we found that they were green. They make rivers run with wine only to make us remember, for one wild moment, that they run with water."[3] Or run with the water of life (pages 62–64).

» Close your eyes and let your imagination run wild for a moment. Describe what you think the New Earth might look like or include. If images are not coming easy, ask God to give you eyes to see a bit of what is to come.

» One of our greatest losses is the gift of wonder, which is the doorway into the kingdom heart. Where have you lost wonder in your life? Can you name when this happened?

Our hearts long to recover a sense of wonder; it is one of the reasons only the child-heart can receive the kingdom. Remember now—we shall be as children again:

"Let the little children come to me, and do not hinder them, for the kingdom of God belongs to such as these. Truly I tell you, anyone who will not receive the kingdom of God like a little child will never enter it" (Mark 10:14–15).

The adult in us says, *How touching*, and dismisses it the next moment in order to go on with our very grown-up lives. But Jesus is being utterly serious, and thank God. For it is the child-heart still in us that loves Mos Eisley, Middle Earth, Narnia—these fairy-tale worlds that in hope-beyond-hope we long to be lost in ourselves. (Thus the allure of video games that let us do so, in an artificial way.) I believe it is right here that we can discern the longing for the kingdom most clearly—the child in us longing for wonder and a "new world"; the promise of the earth in its wildest and most radiant moments whispering back, *It is coming; it's just around the corner.*

This resurrection life you received from God is not a timid, grave-tending life. It's adventurously expectant, greeting God with a childlike "What's next, Papa?" God's Spirit touches our spirits and confirms who we really are. We know who he is, and we know who we are: Father and children. And we know we are going to get what's coming to us—an unbelievable inheritance! We go through exactly what Christ goes through. If we go through the hard times with him, then we're certainly going to go through the good times with him!

That's why I don't think there's any comparison between the present hard times and the coming good times. The created world itself can hardly wait for what's coming next. Everything in creation is being more or less held back. God reins it in until both creation and all the creatures are ready and can be released at the same moment into the glorious times ahead. Meanwhile, the joyful anticipation deepens (Romans 8:15–21 MSG).

"What's next, Papa?" indeed (pages 64–66).

» Do you feel you have a child-heart as described here? Why do you think it's nonnegotiable to Jesus that we must receive the kingdom of God as a child before we can enter into it (see Mark 10:14–15)?

» When is the last time you asked God, "What's next, Papa?" How would your day change if you started each day with this question?

Creation Is Restored

As a boy I loved all things new—a new book, a new bike, new cowboy boots; new lunch box, pocketknife, haircut, friend. Most adults love the "newness" of something new—the smell of a new car, the carpet in a new house. A new song, a new set of your favorite gear, new shoes.... "New year, new you" goes the marketing every January. We all long for a fresh start in a new world.

And you shall have it. For . . . God does not destroy the earth nor his beloved creation; he makes everything brand spanking new. Oh, the *wonder* of it! . . .

Yes—all this shall be ours, a breathtaking world waiting right outside our door when all the earth is restored to its full glory. The return of Jesus may come with the trumpet blast, but what musical score will accompany the restoration of all things? Will it begin quietly, a single oboe, piercing and beautiful and poetic? Will it swell and crescendo to a mighty orchestra? . . .

Oh yes, we will recover wonder. . . .

What will *waterfalls* be like in the New Earth? What of the giant sequoias or tender wildflowers? What will rain be like? And think of your special places; imagine what it will be like to see them in their glory. How sweet it will be to revisit treasured nooks and vistas, gardens and swimming holes again, see them as they truly "are," unveiled, everything God meant them to be. Part of what makes the wonder so precious is that while it is a "new" world, it is *our* world, the world dearest to our hearts, romance at its best (pages 66, 68–69).

» What fresh start do you most look forward to in the New Earth?

» What childhood place would you like to revisit once it has been made new?

Including the Animal Kingdom!

The child-heart wants to know, "Will there be animals in heaven?" and the calloused grown-up heart dismisses the question as theologically unworthy. May I point out that the whole debate ends when you realize that heaven comes to earth; our home is right here on a renewed planet. How could our creative God renew his precious earth and not fill it with a renewed animal kingdom? That would be like a school without children, a village without people. The sheer barrenness and bleakness of the thought is utterly abhorrent to the child-heart of God and his love for the animals, his precious creations.

We know there are horses, for Jesus and his company return on horseback:

> Then I saw Heaven open wide—and oh! a white horse and its Rider. The Rider, named Faithful and True, judges and makes war in pure righteousness. . . . The armies of Heaven, mounted on white horses and dressed in dazzling white linen, follow him (Revelation 19:11–14 MSG). . . .

And then there is this verse in Isaiah:

> The wolf will romp with the lamb,
>   the leopard sleep with the kid.
> Calf and lion will eat from the same trough,
>   and a little child will tend them.
> Cow and bear will graze the same pasture,
>   their calves and cubs grow up together,
>   and the lion eat straw like the ox.
> The nursing child will crawl over rattlesnake dens,
>   the toddler stick his hand down the hole of a serpent.
> Neither animal nor human will hurt or kill
>   on my holy mountain.
> The whole earth will be brimming with knowing God-Alive,
>   a living knowledge of God ocean-deep, ocean-wide
>   (Isaiah 11:6–9 MSG).

Now, unless you want to dismiss this as completely allegorical, we have wolves, lambs, leopards, goats, cows, lions, and bears in the kingdom as well. The passage is clearly describing the kingdom of God operating in its fullness on earth—the renewal of all things. And animals are clearly a part of it, praise our loving Father (pages 70–72).

» Have you wondered if there will be animals or long-gone pets in heaven? How does it feel to know our renewed planet will have a renewed animal kingdom?

» What image or promise stands out to you most in the verse from Isaiah? Why?

But this time around—I can barely write this without trembling—the animal kingdom will be our joyful partners. They will not be afraid of us anymore; they will long to love and serve us. For we were once lords of the animal kingdom, and in the re-created earth we shall take up that beautiful mantle again. . . .

Imagine the animals coming to our call, coming to honor us as their renewed masters. What will it be like to be partners again with nature?

And what does a *restored* rabbit look like? Is he bigger? Faster? Does he bound with greater leaps? What about a restored bear? The bears of this world grow larger the farther north you go; what is the size of a bear in its Eden-glory? Are restored bears more beautiful? Of course they are, and certainly gentle, for "neither animal nor human will hurt or kill on my holy mountain." Imagine—we will be like Noah, as the animals run to us to be reacquainted.

Will your childhood dog run to meet you? (God makes all things new.) Will he be taller, stronger, though every bit his true self? Will his bright eyes have so much to say? . . .

Fully restored humans will have all the intuitive faculties and animal sense to communicate with a bright, intelligent, and restored animal kingdom. And the Holy Spirit will fill every relationship, enabling us to grow in perfect understanding of them and they of us. How could we be their shepherd lords again if we do not "speak" to one another?

My heart just skipped a beat. We are getting close to Narnia indeed. Or perhaps Narnia was simply peeking into the Renewal; I think it will be far more wondrous to "speak" to animals each in their language, rather than have them all speak ours (pages 72–74).

» How does this session expand your vision of God's love for his creatures and their participation in the New Earth?

» Which animals would you love to have a deep and holy friendship with in the New Earth? Why?

Playing in Creation

Creation *wants* to play. My dogs allow me about an hour and a half at the keyboard before they interrupt and insist on a romp. Perhaps you've had the joy of being on a boat in warm waters and seeing the happiness of the dolphins who come to surf the bow wake, making a deliberate choice to drop whatever it was they were doing and come to the sound, come to play on the fringes of our humanity. Nick Jans tells the story of a rare encounter with a black wolf in Juneau, Alaska, who came out of the woods one day on the outskirts of town and played with the dogs locals had brought to run there. Wildlife biologists consider one sighting in a lifetime a success. The wolf hung around for years, showing a keen desire to interact and even play with humans, as if he were a messenger from Eden. . . .[4]

And, friends—I have not even mentioned the angels. Heaven comes to earth, and the angels shall walk in fellowship with man. What do the angels have to teach us? What sort of games do they play? The entire earth will be our playground. I see massive games like lacrosse being played by angels and men across vast landscapes.

This is why you don't need a bucket list. It's all yours, and you can never lose it. Oh, how I long to wander the beautiful places, without a curfew, without the end of vacation always looming. You've longed to see the fjords of Norway? Done. You've secretly hoped to wander the jungles of Africa? Yours too. What next? The Amazon? Antarctica? And I am only touching on the earth. What of the microscopic world? It is as vast as the world we call our own, and we shall explore its mysteries. What of the heavens? They, too, shall be ours. . . .

Good thing we have all the time in the world that has no time to explore and come home and tell the tales. To take up new adventures with those who want to sail the seven seas or climb the peaks of the Andes or range the universe itself (pages 75–77).

» Describe the emotions evoked by the phrase "creation wants to play." From angels to animals to the mysteries of uncharted places, where would you begin?

» How does it feel to let go of your bucket list, knowing that all this is yours and you can never lose it?

Remember—Jesus is the forerunner, the "second Adam." All that he was, we shall be. We will have restored bodies like the body of Christ after his resurrection—able to walk on water and defy certain limits known to us now. "St. Peter for a few seconds walked on the water," wrote C. S. Lewis, "and the day will come when there will be a re-made universe, *infinitely* obedient to the will of glorified and obedient men, when we can do all things, when we shall be those gods that we are described as being in Scripture."[5] I love the picture he gave us of this very possibility toward the end of the Narnian tale *The Last Battle*:

> It was the Unicorn who summed up what everyone was feeling. He stamped his right fore-hoof on the ground and neighed and then cried: "I have come home at last! This is my real country! I belong here. This is the land I have been looking for all my life, though I never knew it till now. The reason why we loved the old Narnia is that it sometimes looked a little like this. Bree-hee-hee! Come further up, come further in!" He shook his mane and sprang forward into a great gallop—a Unicorn's gallop which, in our world, would have carried him out of sight in a few moments. But now a most strange thing happened. Everyone else began to run, and they found, to their astonishment, that they could keep up with him. . . . The air flew in their faces as if they were driving fast in a car without a windscreen. The country flew past

as if they were seeing it from the windows of an express train. Faster and faster they raced, but no one got hot or tired or out of breath. If one could run without getting tired, I don't think one would often want to do anything else. . . . So they ran faster and faster till it was more like flying than running, and even the Eagle overhead was going no faster than they. And they went through winding valley after winding valley and up the steep sides of hills and, faster than ever, down the other sides, following the river and sometimes crossing it and skimming across mountain-lakes as if they were living speedboats.[6]

You think I am being fanciful. I am being utterly serious. I am being as serious as Jesus when he warned that only the child-heart can receive the kingdom. Do you really want to suggest sinful man can create stories and worlds that outshine the worlds God will remake? Careful there. "No eye has seen, no ear has heard, and no mind has imagined what God has prepared for those who love him" (1 Corinthians 2:9 NLT). It was our creative Father who gave us our imaginations; the "visions" we tell in story are often prophetic glimpses into his wondrous realms, and his creative majesty will certainly do ours one better in the world to come (pages 77–79).

» Read the passage from *The Last Battle* aloud. What does the unicorn's invitation in the story to "Come further up, come further in!" mean to you?

» Up until now, has your imagination fallen short to all that awaits us in the coming kingdom? Name something you're looking forward to that previously wasn't on your radar. How does it feel to realize we can't outdream God?

Let's treasure every taste of the promise that comes our way. Let's seek them out with new eyes and let them broaden our kingdom imagination. The things we are discussing are utterly real, friends. Utterly real and the most concrete part of your future.

God reins it in until both creation and all the creatures are ready and can be released at the same moment into the glorious times ahead. Meanwhile, the joyful anticipation deepens (Romans 8:18–21 MSG).

There is a deep and holy connection between creation's release and ours. It waits upon us. Let's explore that next.

THE BIG IDEAS

» Not all hopes are created equally; there are casual hopes, precious hopes, and ultimate hopes.
» Once you accept the truth you will lose everything one way or another—then the Restoration and promise that nothing is lost becomes news beyond your wildest dreams.
» Our hearts long to recover a sense of wonder. Only the child-heart can receive the kingdom.
» Creation wants to play. And it will be fully restored—including the animal kingdom.

GROUP DISCUSSION

Watch the video for session 2. If you find it helpful, use the following space to take a few notes on anything that stood out to you.

Teaching Notes

Discussion Questions

After the teaching session has ended, discuss as a group any or all of the following questions.

1. In the video, I share the story of raising my three boys and how hard it was as one by one they grew up and left for college. What does this story provoke in your heart about seasons of letting go or loss?

2. Having hope is the sign of a heart fully alive. But there is a difference between casual, precious, and ultimate hopes. Briefly share one of your hopes from each category with the group.

3. **Read 1 Peter 3:15** and **Hebrews 6:19.** When was the last time anyone asked you about the reason for the hope you have? How can we make the renewal of all things the ultimate anchor of hope for our soul?

4. It's hard to fathom, but we will all ultimately say good-bye to everyone we love and everything we hold dear. And, yes, each of us will die one day as well. Yet we grasp at every possible means to avoid the inevitable. What kingdom counterfeits and distractions do you give your hopes to rather than face this truth?

5. *Nothing is lost.* That's one of the most powerful promises the world has ever heard. Take a moment and let that sink in. What is the most difficult aspect of that statement to believe? How is God revealing to you that this is true?

6. **Read Romans 8:19–20.** Take a moment to describe what you imagine the world will be like on the morning of its recreation when it is no longer "subjected to frustration . . . by the will of the one who subjected it." Now envision one of your favorite places—perhaps from childhood or family vacations—and share what it may be like on the day it is transformed.

7. **Read Isaiah 11:6–7.** What does the thought of a restored animal kingdom stir in your heart? Does the thought of communicating with them sound too surreal? Why?

GROUP EXERCISE

Each person will need a pen and a sheet of paper for this exercise. Write "My Bucket List" at the top and list all the things you feel pressure to do before you "kick the bucket." After you read it aloud, rip your paper into pieces to symbolize your freedom from such a list. Discuss how it feels to know we can see and do everything we've dreamed of—with no time or physical limits—in the New Earth.

YOUR STORY TOLD RIGHTLY

I had a dream about Craig a few nights ago

I was at some sort of gathering, filled with people from our community. I'm not sure if it was an "earthly" event or a kingdom one. It felt simply ordinary.

But then again.

I looked to my right, and across the room I saw Craig. He was standing there talking to someone, as if he'd never been away.

In my dream I burst into tears. I've never done that in a dream before.

—JOHN ELDREDGE, *All Things New*

Personal Preparation

This week, read chapters 5 and 6 in *All Things New:* "Our Restoration" and "When Every Story Is Told Rightly." Let's begin again simply with your reaction to the chapters. What did this content stir in you?

Our Restoration

I had a surprising emotional breakthrough the weekend my father died.

Like for many people, my relationship with my dad was kind of a mixed bag. My boyhood days were very precious. My father loved the outdoors, and we did a lot of camping and fishing together; I have golden memories of those days. But then the fall of man caught up with him: a series of lost jobs, followed by the drinking; then a stroke; then cancer; finally that brutal mocker, dementia. He spent his last days in a small convalescent facility in Southern California, then came home for hospice.

He died on Father's Day weekend, of all sad things. . . .

So much had been lost; so much irrecoverable. The sun was just coming over the mountains, and the irrigation ditch was bubbling next to me like a brook; the meadowlarks called to one another across the lush hay fields. It was not a melancholy scene at all. As I gazed on the flowing water rippling over water grasses, I thought of a scene in *The Silver Chair.*

Toward the end of the story, the children sent to Narnia find themselves once again high on Aslan's mountain. King Caspian has died, and even though they have left that sad scene back on the quay, the funeral music is still somehow playing around them:

They were walking beside the stream and the Lion went before them: and he became so beautiful, and the music so despairing, that Jill did not know which of them it was that filled her eyes with tears.

Then Aslan stopped, and the children looked into the stream. And there, on the golden gravel of the bed of the stream, lay King Caspian, dead, with the water flowing over him like liquid glass. His long white beard swayed in it like water weed. And all three stood and wept. Even the lion wept: great Lion-tears, each tear more precious than the Earth would be if it was a single solid diamond. . . .

"Son of Adam," said Aslan, "go into that thicket and pluck the thorn that you will find there and bring it to me." Eustace obeyed. The thorn was a foot long and sharp as a rapier. "Drive it into my paw, son of Adam," said Aslan, holding up his right fore-paw and spreading out the great pad toward Eustace. "Must I?" said Eustace. "Yes," said Aslan.

Then Eustace set his teeth and drove the thorn into the Lion's pad. And there came out a great drop of blood, redder than all redness that you have ever seen or imagined. And it splashed into the stream over the dead body of the King. At the same moment the doleful music stopped. And the dead King began to be changed. His white beard turned to gray, and from gray to yellow, and got shorter and vanished all together; and his sunken cheeks grew round and fresh, and the wrinkles were smoothed, and his eyes opened, and his eyes and lips both laughed, and suddenly he leapt up and stood before them—a very young man. . . . And he rushed to Aslan and flung his arms as far as they would go round the huge neck; and he gave Aslan the strong kisses of a King, and Aslan gave him the wild kisses of a lion.[7]

This moment is yours, as sure and certain as God himself. Sure as the renewal of heaven and earth. How else could we enjoy the fierce beauty of a renewed creation unless we, too, are renewed and made strong, stronger than we ever were here? How could we possibly play in the fields of a New Earth or fulfill our roles in the kingdom of God unless we are, well—glorious (*All Things New*, pages 82–86)?

» How does this scene from *The Silver Chair* cause you to consider death in a new way?

» "How else could we enjoy the fierce beauty of a renewed creation unless we, too, are renewed and made strong, stronger than we ever were here? How could we possibly play in the fields of a New Earth or fulfill our roles in the kingdom of God unless we are, well—glorious?" What do you feel these words are inviting you to consider . . . perhaps for the first time?

Forever Young

> He wraps you in goodness—beauty eternal.
> He renews your youth—you're always young in
> his presence (Psalm 103:4–5 MSG). . . .

Youth is what enables us to enjoy life. No, that's not quite right; *youthfulness* is what enables us to find the wonder in everything. Vibrancy. Lighthearted, like you feel late into a long vacation. Hopeful, like a child on Christmas morning. The absence of all cynicism and resignation—not to mention all physical suffering.

I love that part in *The Silver Chair* when old age simply vanishes from frail King Caspian, because age is the unavoidable meltdown, stripping even the bravest and most beautiful of their former glory. Whatever physical affliction you have known, whatever your limitations have been, everything old age will eventually strip you of—it will all be washed away. Your renewed body will be like the body of Jesus. We will burst forth into the new creation like children let out for summer break, running, somersaulting, cartwheeling into the meadows of the New Earth. Running like the children, "without getting tired . . . faster and faster till it was more like flying than running, and even the Eagle overhead was going no faster than they" (pages 86, 90).

» How would you describe the difference between "youth" and "youthfulness"?

» Do you feel more resignation or vibrancy in this season of life? Explain.

» "Everything old age will eventually strip you of will one day simply be washed away." What does this statement do for your heart? If you are relatively young, consider what this means for a parent or elderly friend.

Our Internal Restoration

> "'He will wipe every tear from their eyes. There will be no more death' or mourning or crying or pain, for the old order of things has passed away."
>
> He who was seated on the throne said, "I am making everything new!" (Revelation 21:4–5)

No more tears. No more pain. No more death. No longer any reason to mourn. At the renewal of all things, our hearts are going to be free from grief. The joy of this will far surpass our physical relief. Think of it—if God would offer today to remove from you just one of your greatest sources of internal pain, what would you ask him to remove?

And once it were gone, what would your joy be like? . . .

And if *all* your brokenness were finally and completely healed, and all your sin removed from you as far as the east is from the west (see Psalm 103:12)—what will you no longer face? What will you finally be? How about your loved ones— what will they no longer wrestle with? What do they finally get to be?

We shall, finally and fully, be *wholehearted*—a wish so deep in my soul I can hardly speak it (page 91).

» What one source of internal pain would you most like God to remove today?

» How would that transform you on a physical level? What about from a spiritual perspective?

» Think of who you will finally get to be on the day all your sin is removed and your brokenness is completely healed. How would you describe that person?

I was holding our new granddaughter the other night on my knees, such a tiny and fragile thing. And my heart was pierced for her because I know what hell this world can unleash on a tender heart. The human heart and soul are imbued with a remarkable resilience. But they are also very fragile, for we were made for the habitat of Eden and not the desolation of war in which we now live. When the promised Messiah is foretold in Isaiah, the center of his work is clearly named—he will come to heal all our inner brokenness:

> The Spirit of the Sovereign LORD is on me,
>   because the LORD has anointed me
>   to proclaim good news to the poor.
> He has sent me to bind up the brokenhearted,
>   to proclaim freedom for the captives
>   and release from darkness for the prisoners (Isaiah 61:1).

The Hebrew for "brokenhearted" is a conjunction of two words: *leb*, which is the heart, and *shabar*, a word that means "broken" or "to break, to rend violently." Isaiah elsewhere uses *shabar* to describe dry branches that are broken into pieces, or statues that have fallen off their pedestals and shattered upon the ground. *Shabar* refers to a *literal* breaking, the shattering of the human heart. As if I had to explain this to you; a tender and compassionate look into your own soul will show you exactly what I am talking about. . . .

And our Healer will make us whole again. The little boy or girl in you who has so long hidden in fear, the angry adolescent, the heartbroken man or woman—all of "you" will be brought home to you, a fully integrated human being. "At such a time, we will be fully integrated once again—body, mind, spirit, and soul—just as we were intended to live with God at the beginning of creation."[8]

And there is more.

> You have come to Mount Zion, to the city of the living God, the heavenly Jerusalem, and to countless thousands of angels in a joyful gathering. You have

come to the assembly of God's firstborn children,
whose names are written in heaven. You have come
to God himself, who is the judge over all things. You
have come to the spirits of the righteous ones in
heaven who have now been made perfect (Hebrews
12:22–23 NLT).

That phrase "the righteous ones . . . made perfect." I can
hardly speak. Finally, the totality of our being will be saturated only with goodness. Think of it—think of all that you're
not going to have to wrestle with anymore. The fear that has
been your lifelong battle, the anger, the compulsions, the
battles to forgive, that nasty root of resentment. No more
internal civil wars; no doubt, no lust, no regret; no shame, no
self-hatred, no gender confusion. What has plagued you all
your life? Your Healer will personally lift it from your shoulders (pages 91–95).

» Have you considered the primary reason Jesus came was to heal
our broken hearts and set us free (see Isaiah 61:1)? What does
that say about the central importance of your internal restoration to Jesus?

» What thoughts or temptations have plagued you recently—or
perhaps all your life? Now imagine being saturated only with
goodness—and how you'll no longer wrestle with those issues
again. Describe what that will be like.

Seeing Our Loved Ones Restored

It may be a difficult thing for you to imagine, your soul's complete restoration. But perhaps we can get there when we
think of the restoration of the ones we love. Think of the joy
it will be to see your spouse, your dearest friend, your son or
daughter no longer fighting their internal battles. To see them
young and well, alive and free, everything you knew they
were! You always knew there was a radiance, a trueness, a
shining greatness in there, though they never could quite take
hold of it for themselves. And you *see* it. How many times over
will we hear at the feast, "Look at you! You're glorious!"? . . .

Whom do you look forward to seeing again? We're all
going to be at the wedding feast, for we are each of us guests
of honor at that banquet. We get Bilbo's party. Put that on
your bathroom mirror: *We get Bilbo's party!* Just think of the
joy in all the reunions that will take place! . . .

After that . . . think of the storytelling! . . .

Think of it—a hush comes over the wedding feast as certain guests are called forward to tell the Great Stories. Moses
recounts the flight from Egypt and the parting of the sea.
David comes forth to reenact his battle with Goliath. Mary
steps forward (will she be clothed with the sun?) and tells
stories from the hidden days of Jesus' boyhood. A murmur
of excitement ripples through the crowd as Adam and Eve
step forward and rather bashfully tell the story of naming the
animals (they had a few disagreements that had to be sorted
out over the hedgehog and the narwhal).

And no one will grow tired, no one will need to head off
to bed. For we will be young, and whole, and filled with Life
(pages 97–100).

» Think of those you most love and what they will be like after
they are completely restored. Now imagine one of them standing

before you. How would you describe them in their full glory—
healed, alive, and free?

» Whom do you look forward to seeing again at the Wedding
Feast? Why?

» Of everyone there, which two people would you most like to sit
next to? What stories from them are you most eager to hear?

Wonder and Our Healing

In his highly researched book *Last Child in the Woods*, Richard Louv documents how postmodern human beings suffer
badly the physical and mental harms of "nature deficit dis-
order."[9] Our lives have become cut off from the Garden we
were meant to flourish in.

Children actually need to play in the dirt to develop some
of the friendly bacteria the human body needs. Evidence is
mounting that many immune deficiency disorders are actually caused because we live in too sterile an environment. A
short walk in the woods reduces your cortisol stress levels.
Isn't it sweet of God that sunshine gives us vitamin D; people
always say how sunshine makes them happy. It actually does.
Patients with windows looking out on nature recover at far

higher rates than those who have no view. Nature heals, dear ones; nature heals. God has ordained that in the New Earth it is *river* water that brings us life and *leaves* that are used for our healing:

> Then the angel showed me a river with the water of life, clear as crystal, flowing from the throne of God and of the Lamb. It flowed down the center of the main street. On each side of the river grew a tree of life, bearing twelve crops of fruit, with a fresh crop each month. The leaves were used for medicine to heal the nations (Revelation 22:1–2 NLT).

Think of the sensual experiences of a restored you in a restored world. What will the aromas be?

Perhaps you've walked through a pine forest on a warm day; if you get up close to the bark, especially on a ponderosa, it smells like butterscotch. My grandmother used to put butterscotch on our ice cream. Can you imagine a whole forest filled with it? I remember the orange groves in Southern California in bloom—such a sweet and lovely scent. I expect the orchards near the city of God will wash the feast in lovely fragrances. My grandfather's ranch was situated in a valley where some folks grew fields of mint; the smell when they harvested was glorious, the whole valley smelled of mojitos or Christmas. We now understand more how fragrances actually affect the brain and facilitate healing. The aromas of the New Earth will bring our healing too.

And what about the sounds of the new Eden? Even now the music of rushing water soothes my soul; I love to sit by babbling brooks, fall asleep to the sound of ocean waves. Just last night two owls were hooting back and forth to each other in our woods; it made my tired soul lighter somehow. We will hear nature in full chorus. It will mingle with the laughter and music and aromas of the feast itself, and we will wander in and out, drinking it all in, practically swimming in the healing powers of creation, feeling Life permeate every last corner of our being. Happiness and joy will overcome us; sorrow and its sighing will vanish forever (pages 100–102).

» How would you describe the healing effects of nature in your life? If you don't tend to spend much time outdoors, why is that?

» Close your eyes and use your senses to imagine the new Eden. What are some of the sights, sounds, smells, and tastes coming from this restored Paradise?

When Every Story Is Told Rightly

Let us return to that stunning passage with which we began our explorations of the *palingenesia*:

> "Truly I tell you, at the renewal of all things, when the Son of Man sits on his glorious throne . . . everyone who has left houses or brothers or sisters or father or mother or wife or children or fields for my sake will receive a hundred times as much and will inherit eternal life" (Matthew 19:28–29).

Jesus was responding to a question when he declared these bold promises. The question came from Peter, though you get the feeling the other fellows put him up to it:

Then Peter said to him, "We've given up everything to follow you. What will we get?" (19:27 NLT).

Christ is neither alarmed nor offended by Peter's question. He doesn't tell him that service is enough, nor that virtue is its own reward. He quickly replies with the proclamation of the Great Renewal, and then—as though that were not enough (!)—goes on to assure the boys that they will be handsomely rewarded in the coming kingdom. A hundredfold. That's a pretty staggering return; perhaps Jesus is simply using hyperbole. But then there is his teaching on the minas and the talents:

> "A man of noble birth went to a distant country to have himself appointed king and then to return. So he called ten of his servants and gave them ten minas. 'Put this money to work,' he said, 'until I come back.'
>
> "But his subjects hated him and sent a delegation after him to say, 'We don't want this man to be our king.'
>
> "He was made king, however, and returned home. Then he sent for the servants to whom he had given the money, in order to find out what they had gained with it.
>
> "The first one came and said, 'Sir, your mina has earned ten more.'
>
> "'Well done, my good servant!' his master replied. 'Because you have been trustworthy in a very small matter, take charge of ten cities.'
>
> "The second came and said, 'Sir, your mina has earned five more.'
>
> "His master answered, 'You take charge of five cities'" (Luke 19:12–19).

The allegory is hardly veiled. Clearly, Jesus is the man of noble birth who left to have himself appointed king (which took place at his ascension) and will return. Upon his return, he rewards his faithful servants (that would be us, his followers). He repeats the promise but ups the ante in the tale of the sheep and goats: "Come, you who are blessed by my Father; take your inheritance, the kingdom prepared for you since the creation of the world" (Matthew 25:31–36). We've gone from houses to cities to kingdoms. We are given *kingdoms*. Which helps to make sense of why we are said to reign with him. More on that in a moment. For now, can you see the theme here? The victorious king gladly rewards his faithful companions (pages 109–111).

» In the New Earth, you may be in charge of a literal kingdom. What does that thought stir in you?

» Do you look forward to the rewards described here with eager anticipation? If so, which sound the most appealing to you? If not—or if this sounds too good to be true—try to put words to that as well.

Reward Is a Kingdom Mind-set

Because our poverty is so great, it would do us good to let the repetition of Scripture open our eyes to how central reward is to a kingdom mind-set:

"Rejoice and be glad, because great is your reward in heaven" (Matthew 5:12).

"Be careful not to practice your righteousness in front of others to be seen by them. If you do, you will have no reward from your Father in heaven. . . . But when you give to the needy, do not let your left hand know what your right hand is doing, so that your giving may be in secret. Then your Father, who sees what is done in secret, will reward you" (Matthew 6:1–4).

"Store up for yourselves treasures in heaven" (Matthew 6:20).

"Whoever welcomes a prophet as a prophet will receive a prophet's reward, and whoever welcomes a righteous person as a righteous person will receive a righteous person's reward" (Matthew 10:41).

"For the Son of Man is going to come in his Father's glory with his angels, and then he will reward each person according to what they have done" (Matthew 16:27).

Serve wholeheartedly, as if you were serving the Lord, not people, because you know that the Lord will reward each one for whatever good they do, whether they are slave or free (Ephesians 6:7–8).

Whatever you do, work at it with all your heart, as working for the Lord, not for human masters, since you know that you will receive an inheritance from the Lord as a reward (Colossians 3:23–24).

So do not throw away your confidence; it will be richly rewarded (Hebrews 10:35).

By faith Moses . . . chose to be mistreated along with the people of God rather than to enjoy the fleeting pleasures of sin. He regarded disgrace for the sake of Christ as of greater value than the treasures of Egypt, because he was looking ahead to his reward (Hebrews 11:24–26).

The biblical canon ends with Jesus making this final statement:

"Look, I am coming soon! My reward is with me, and I will give to each person according to what they have done" (Revelation 22:12). . . .

Oh yes, rewards will be given out in the kingdom with great honor and ceremony. And I believe one of our greatest joys will be to witness it happen.

When you think of all the stories of the saints through the ages, and all the beautiful, heroic, painful, utterly sacrificial choices made by those saints, the suffering, the persecution—how long will we enjoy hearing the stories of those that ought to be rewarded, and then watch breathlessly as our King meets the specific situation with perfect generosity (pages 112–114, 116)?

» Which Scripture jumps out at you as the most compelling regarding rewards? Why?

» For which of your friends and loved ones would you like a front-row seat to witness the bestowing of their rewards? Explain why.

Your Story Told Rightly

Victor Hugo's epic *Les Misérables* has obviously touched something deep in our humanity; there have been three different film versions and one massively successful Broadway musical done in my lifetime. I believe the enduring appeal of the story is that the promise is the overarching theme. The close of the musical and most recent film is an incredibly moving scene where all those who have died are back, singing the great anthem about how we will all be free and live in God's garden and every soul will receive their reward. It is a scene of the great *palingenesia!* No wonder the musical has been wildly popular.

But there is something else—the power of a story told rightly. Jean Valjean is such a good man, but fate has dealt him an unjust hand. He is a hunted man, misunderstood, maligned, having to flee one city to the next all his life. But *we* see his great heart, his sacrificial choices, and at the end we see he is finally vindicated—how he did the most loving and sacrificial thing, how his life was actually filled with beauty and dignity. The great cloud of witnesses shows up for his arrival into the kingdom of heaven and he deserves it.

Oh, how we ache for this moment, each one of us. . . .

How do you tell the story of a human life? How can you do justice to all the hidden sorrow, the valiant fighting, the millions of small, unseen choices, the impact of a great soul on thousands of other lives? How can you begin to say what a life means to the kingdom of God?

The answer is, only *in* the kingdom of God. Only once we are there. Your story will be told rightly. . . .

How wonderful it will be to see Jesus Christ vindicated, after so many eons of mockery, dismissal, and vilification. Our Beloved has endured such slander, such mistrust, and, worst of all, such grotesque distortion by the caricatures and

religious counterfeits paraded in his name. All the world will
see him *as he is*, see him crowned King. Every tongue will
be silenced, and his vindication will bring tremendous joy to
those who love him!

But friends—that vindication is also yours. . . .

All those decisions your family misinterpreted and the
accusations you bore, the many ways you paid for it. The
thousands of unseen choices to overlook a cutting remark,
a failure, to be kind to that friend who failed you again. The
things that you wish you had personally done better, but at
the time no one knew what you were laboring under—the
warfare, the depression, the chronic fatigue. The millions of
ways you have been missed and terribly misunderstood. Your
Defender will make it all perfectly clear; you will be vindicated
(pages 117–119).

» In order for our lives to be rewarded, we need our stories to be
told and told rightly. What do you most look forward to regarding this moment?

» Do you find fear trying to enter into this scenario? That's understandable, since this idea has often been set within the context of
judgment and justice that will be served. But remember that our
every sin is forgiven, and we live under mercy. There is no condemnation now for those who are in Christ (see Romans 8:1). If
you are still wrestling with this issue, write your concerns below
and ask God to replace fear with joy for this time of reward (see
1 Corinthians 3:10–14).

Envisioning Your Homecoming

What do you want your reception in the kingdom to look like? Have you even thought about it? . . .

Perhaps it is only a boyish desire (but remember, only the child-heart receives the kingdom), yet I love the stories where acts of courage are celebrated. . . .

There is a scene toward the end of *The Return of the King*, when dear Sam and Frodo—rescued from the fires of Mount Doom—have awakened to find themselves in the forest of Ithilien. Gandalf leads them through the beautiful woods toward the camp of Aragorn, now the king of Gondor:

> As they came to the opening in the wood, they were surprised to see knights in bright mail and tall guards in silver and black standing there, who greeted them with honour and bowed before them. And then one blew a long trumpet, and they went on through the aisle of trees beside the singing stream. So they came to a wide green land, and beyond it was a broad river in a silver haze, out of which rose a long wooded isle, and many ships lay by its shores. But on the field where they now stood a great host was drawn up, in ranks and companies glittering in the sun. And as the Hobbits approached swords were unsheathed, and spears were shaken, and horns and trumpets sang.[10]

Doesn't it bring tears to your eyes, knowing how much they have been through to deserve that moment? They more than deserve that moment, and it fills my own heart with longing for such a reception into the kingdom. . . .

A friend of mine who has labored long in the Great War with evil shared his vision with me in a moment of tender vulnerability:

I want to finish well. I want to return as a hero, a warrior worthy of the kingdom. I had this vision—I don't know if it was an actual vision or just my heart's expression. I saw myself, sword at my side, shield slung over my back, making my way up the main street of the City. I wore the battle gear of war, soiled by long years at the front. People lined both sides of the street to welcome me, the great cloud, I guess; I recognized hundreds of faces, the faces of those whose freedom I fought for. Their smiles and tears filled my heart with profound joy. As I made my way up the street toward Jesus and our Father, my friends and fellow warriors stepped into the street with me, and we moved forward as a band. I saw angels there, maybe the angels who fought for us and with us, walking alongside. I saw flower petals on the pavement; I saw banners flapping in the breeze. We reached the throne and knelt. Jesus came forward and kissed my forehead, and we embraced deeply, freely, like I always knew we would. Then my Father stepped forward and took me by the shoulders and said, "Well done, my son. Very well done indeed. Welcome home." As we embraced, a great cheer went up from the crowd.

Now, that would be a reception worth living for. The reality that every story will be told rightly should affect your choices today. If there is no cost to our Christian faith, how then shall we be rewarded (pages 122–127)?

» Perhaps the reason you have been losing heart is because you didn't know the great rewards that are just around the corner for you. Pause and think about it. This place in your heart needs to be *filled* with rich images of real anticipation; this was meant to be the fuel that sustains your long journey here. What specific rewards are you banking everything on?

» What would you love your reception into the kingdom to be? You should put some words to that, given how important it is.

If we would also like to receive a hero's welcome after laboring long in our Great War with evil, it helps to keep in mind that valiant deeds require desperate times. The desperate times are all around us, friends; now for the valiant deeds. We will look at this next.

THE BIG IDEAS

» Our internal restoration is one of the greatest gifts we will receive when all things are made new. We shall finally and fully be *wholehearted*.

» The earth waits for our healing, and we await the earth's healing.

» Reward is a kingdom mind-set. Our desires aren't too great but too small.

» In the coming kingdom, our stories will be told rightly and we will be vindicated.

GROUP DISCUSSION

Watch the video for session 3. If you find it helpful, use the following space to take a few notes on anything that stood out to you.

Teaching Notes

Discussion Questions

After the teaching session has ended, discuss as a group any or all
of the following questions.

1. **Read Romans 8:21.** Why do you think creation is waiting on
   its restoration until our restoration occurs?

2. Imagine seeing friends and family who, in the New Earth, finally have everlasting joy. They are whole, alive, and everything
   you knew they were always meant to be. What will that be like?
   Now consider how your own internal restoration will transform you at the renewal of all things. What you will be most
   excited to finally be free of or healed from?

3. **Read Revelation 21:3–4.** Which promise or phrase from this
   passage most captures your heart? Why?

4. Which stories are you most looking forward to hearing in person at the Wedding Feast? Stories from Creation? The battle
   of David and Goliath? Jesus walking on water? Or perhaps
   stories from your family tree that happened long before you
   were born? Along with naming the stories, share why those
   particular ones hold such meaning.

5. In the video, you learned the significance of every story being
   told rightly. What facts or situations from your life are you
   eager to have shared and interpreted in all their completeness
   and trueness?

6. **Read Matthew 19:27–29.** What do you think it will look like
   for those who made sacrifices for Jesus to receive—in addition
   to eternal life—everything restored a hundred times over? Try
   to describe this as tangibly and practically as possible.

7. When Jesus is crowned King, we will finally see him as he is. Jesus will be vindicated. His story will be told rightly. What about this moment are you most anticipating? Why?

GROUP EXERCISE

Reward, reward, reward—it fills the pages of both Testaments. Saint Paul expected to be rewarded for his service to Christ, as have the saints down through the ages. Patrick, that mighty missionary to the Irish, prayed daily, "In the hope of resurrection to meet with reward. . . . So that there may come to me an abundance of reward."[11] It is our barren age that is out of sync with the tradition.

C. S. Lewis wrote:

> If we consider the unblushing promises of reward and the staggering nature of the rewards promised in the Gospels, it would seem that Our Lord finds our desires not too strong, but too weak. We are half-hearted creatures, fooling about with drink and sex and ambition when infinite joy is offered us, like an ignorant child who wants to go on making mud pies in a slum because he cannot imagine what is meant by the offer of a holiday at the sea.[12]

Discuss as a group this thought that God finds our desires not too strong but too weak. Do you find this to be true personally? If so, how might you strengthen your desires for the rewards your good Father wants to bestow upon you?

WHAT WE'LL DO IN THE NEW EARTH

"Gandalf! I thought you were dead! But then I thought I was dead myself. Is everything sad going to come untrue? What's happened to the world?"

"A great Shadow has departed," said Gandalf, and then he laughed and the sound was like music, or like water in a parched land; and as he listened the thought came to Sam that he had not heard laughter, the pure sound of merriment, for days upon days without count. It fell upon his ears like the echo of all the joys he had ever known.

—J. R. R. TOLKIEN, *The Lord of the Rings*

PERSONAL PREPARATION

This week, read chapters 7 and 8 in *All Things New*: "The Overthrow of Evil" and "What Do We Actually Do?" Let's begin again simply with your reaction to the chapters. What did this content stir in you?

The Overthrow of Evil

Once upon a time the earth was whole and beautiful, shimmering like an emerald, filled with glory, bursting with *anticipation*. Such wonders waiting to be unveiled, such adventures waiting to be ours. Creation was a fairy tale, a great legend—only true.

Once upon a time we were whole and beautiful too, glorious, striding through the Garden like the sons and daughters of God. A daughter of God is a goddess; a son of God is a god. "I said, 'You are "gods"; you are all sons of the Most High'" (Psalm 82:6). We were holy and powerful; we ruled the earth and animal kingdom with loving-kindness.

But Eden was vulnerable; something dark slithered in the shadows. Something most foul and sinister. Banished from heaven, Satan and his fallen warriors came seeking revenge. . . .

If the coming Restoration is to be fulfilled on the earth and in our lives, Satan and his armies must be destroyed. He must never be allowed in again.

We are letting the great stories awaken our imaginations to the coming kingdom, fill our hearts with brilliant images and hopeful expectation. Let us seize the moment crucial to the climax of every story and the redemption we long to see: that glorious moment when evil is defeated (*All Things New*, pages 129–131).

» Pause and let this be true: evil will be judged, and Satan, his armies, and every form of evil will be destroyed with a punishment that never ends, under justice unrelenting. Does it feel like a ten-ton weight has just been lifted off your being? What will this moment mean for you?

» What do you imagine it will feel like when the human race will be whole and glorious once more, striding through the New Earth as the sons and daughters of God?

Our Story

Oh, the joy we will experience when we get to watch with our own eyes the Enemy brought down for good, cast into his eternal torment! Oh, the hope that begins to rise at the thought of a world where the Enemy no longer gets to do what he does. To see our loved ones released from their lifelong battles. To be released from our own lifelong battles, knowing with utter surety that the kingdom of death and darkness is forever destroyed.

This is my favorite scene in the film *The Last of the Mohicans*, a story set in the French and Indian War of the mid-1700s. It was a vicious war, with savagery practiced on both sides. In the film the archvillain is a very twisted character, the Huron Indian named Magua. His mind and heart are so tormented with bitterness and bloodlust, he gives himself over to become wickedness incarnate. Magua is a betrayer and murderer; he destroys the lives and happiness of many people.

The Mohawk warrior Chingachgook is the father figure in the film, like our heavenly Father. He has two sons—Uncas, his son by birth, and Nathanial, his adopted white son. Late in the film Magua has cut out the heart of an English captain and taken his two daughters as slaves; the daughters are each the love of one of Chingachgook's sons. (The bride taken captive, just as in our story.) The three warriors, father and sons, race to rescue them. Uncas reaches Magua first, but Magua is powerful; he kills the beautiful young Indian warrior and throws him off a cliff. His love, Alice, throws herself off behind him rather than become Magua's sexual slave. Then the father arrives and takes his revenge. Magua is brought down; Chingachgook kills him with his battle-ax.

The evil one finally gets what he deserves; he is stopped, judged, and destroyed. Every time I see a scene like that, I remind Satan that this is his end. *This is coming*, I think. *This is your end*.

You long for this day, and you long for it in very particular ways (pages 135–136).

» Imagine all the physical affliction, emotional torment, abuse—all the evil in this world—has vanished. Consider what it will be like to no longer be assaulted by Satan. To be utterly free from accusation; to look in the mirror and hear no accusing thoughts or voices. To be completely free of all temptation and the sabotage of your character—not because you are successfully resisting it in a moment of great resolve, but because it is *no longer in existence* anywhere in the world. What evils will you personally no longer have to live with?

» Describe what it will be like to have the veil fully lifted that so often clouds our relationship with Jesus.

A Heart for Redemption

Some stories and images stay in your mind for years; sadly, it is usually the darker ones. I remember leafing through a catalog of WWII photos when I came across one I could not stop looking at. At first all I saw was a large group of soldiers milling about; then I realized they were standing in a few long lines, smoking and chatting like soldiers waiting to get into the mess hall or use the latrine. I looked down at the inscription, which explained this mob of Japanese soldiers was waiting their turn with Korean "comfort girls," young captive women forced to have sex with hundreds of enemies every day.

I nearly threw up; I could even now as I tell you this. I wanted to scream; I wanted to do something about it.

The human race has showed itself capable of unspeakable evils at war. But war is now at our doorstep, and this practice has become a major global industry. Millions of human beings—including children—are forced into sexual acts every day on this planet; $186 billion is spent on prostitution worldwide annually.[13] Friends of mine who minister to the victims report that the stories they are hearing now are far more heinous than they were even ten years ago. . . .

Now read this passage:

> After this I saw another angel coming down from heaven. He had great authority, and the earth was illuminated by his splendor. With a mighty voice he shouted:
>
> > "'Fallen! Fallen is Babylon the Great!'
> > She has become a dwelling for demons
> > and a haunt for every impure spirit,
> >   a haunt for every unclean bird,
> >   a haunt for every unclean and detestable animal.
> > For all the nations have drunk
> >   the maddening wine of her adulteries.
> > The kings of the earth committed adultery with her,
> >   and the merchants of the earth grew rich from her
> >   excessive luxuries" (Revelation 18:1–3).

Human sin is not sufficient to explain the rampaging, unspeakable evil of this age. There are powerful, ancient dark spirits—those same fallen angels who invaded Eden—who are now deeply involved ensnaring, entrapping, fueling evil people, making war on holiness and on the human heart. The Whore of Babylon is the one behind the sex trade in all its dark corruptions; Scripture says she has made the world "drunk [with] the maddening wine of her adulteries" (Revelation 18:3) (pages 137–139).

» The torment of living in an evil age is traumatizing to the soul. What has that done to your heart?

» Truly, an intoxicated sexual madness has come over the earth. Describe your thoughts on what is happening in Revelation 18:1–3.

The Whore of Babylon is going to be severely judged by our righteous Lord:

> "Give back to her as she has given;
>   pay her back double for what she has done.
>   Pour her a double portion from her own cup.
> Give her as much torment and grief
>   as the glory and luxury she gave herself.
> In her heart she boasts,
>   'I sit enthroned as queen.
> I am not a widow;
>   I will never mourn.'
> Therefore in one day her plagues will overtake her:
>   death, mourning and famine.
> She will be consumed by fire,
>   for mighty is the Lord God who judges her."

"When the kings of the earth who committed adultery with her and shared her luxury see the smoke of her burning, they will weep and mourn over her. Terrified at her torment, they will stand far off and cry:

> "'Woe! Woe to you, great city,
>   you mighty city of Babylon!
> In one hour your doom has come!'" (Revelation 18:6–10).

This passage fills me with such relief, anticipation, and something like holy revenge. Think of every little girl and boy forced to have sex with corrupt adults; think of every woman and man drugged and held captive as sexual slaves. Think of the *shattering* of those human hearts. Now think of the shout that will go up when the Whore is cast down forever:

After this I heard what sounded like the roar of a great multitude in heaven shouting:

> "Hallelujah!
> Salvation and glory and power belong to our God,
>> for true and just are his judgments.
> He has condemned the great prostitute
>> who corrupted the earth by her adulteries.
> He has avenged on her the blood of his servants."

And again they shouted:

> "Hallelujah!
> The smoke from her goes up for ever and ever."

The twenty-four elders and the four living creatures fell down and worshiped God, who was seated on the throne. And they cried:

> "Amen, Hallelujah!"

Then a voice came from the throne, saying:
> "Praise our God,
>> all you his servants,
> you who fear him,
>> both great and small!"

Then I heard what sounded like a great multitude, like the roar of rushing waters and like loud peals of thunder, shouting:

"Hallelujah!
   For our Lord God Almighty reigns.
Let us rejoice and be glad
   and give him glory!
For the wedding of the Lamb has come,
   and his bride has made herself ready.
Fine linen, bright and clean,
    was given her to wear" (Revelation 19:1–8).

Won't it be marvelous to hear that roar of rushing waters, the triumphant shout like thunder from the hosts of the kingdom? You will hear that shout, friends; you will join it with all the power of your lungs (pages 139–141).

» Think of all the justice that needs to be served. You have particular passions for justice and redemption, and they will be realized. Your heart needs to know this—they *will* be realized. What is the redemption your heart longs for on a global level?

» What cause or passion tugs at your heart? Are you drawn to a particular community or national plight? To specific arts and sciences? Explain.

» You have special longings for the redemption of those close to you. They were given to you by the God who shares them, and they, too, *will* be fulfilled. What is the redemption your heart aches for on a personal level? What cries fill your prayers in the night?

Justice Will Be Served

We preach a gospel of mercy. But it is mercy bought at a terrible price. We are saved from the judgment of God, not because he decided to toss justice in the gutter, but because he poured it out upon his own Son on the cross. That mercy is being extended to all mankind—so long as we are in *this* age. But when the Day of the Lord arrives, justice will be served. A day of reckoning is coming, and we need it to be so. . . .

This is where Hinduism, Buddhism, and other religions that deny or ignore the actual, personal existence of evil fall so short. (Branches of Christianity have done the same.) Without naming evil for exactly what it is, and without a day of reckoning, there can be no justice.

Imagine, friends, a world without evil. Every demon has been swept away. I will say more about who shares in the Great Restoration in session 5, but for now simply imagine a world without evil people, where everyone loves God and overflows with his holy love. You look to your right and left, and you only see people you can trust completely. Lot's torment will no longer be ours; holiness will permeate all things. No wonder joy is the constant mood of the kingdom! Not to mention massive relief and vindication too (pages 144–145).

» Do you think the promise of justice fulfilled is one of the great hopes of the coming kingdom? Why or why not?

» What will it be like to live in a world without evil? Name some ways daily life will look different when there are no crimes, attacks, war, revenge, or hate.

Our Longing Will Be Fulfilled

I believe we have a role to play in the administration of justice when the evil one and all in his service are sentenced. We will be there when our Lord judges the evil that has oppressed our family. We will be called forward as witnesses for the prosecution. We will preside with him when justice is carried out on the evil that has been behind those causes dear to us—poverty, abuse, racism, human trafficking, and the destruction of the earth itself.

Intimate and personal justice will be granted to us as well. . . . I know that so much has been stolen in my life. So many blessings, so many gifts, so much taken from my relationships, opportunities, personal restoration that was diminished or thwarted. You have too, dear ones—so much has been stolen from you. And it will be repaid a hundredfold. This recompense, this restitution must be part of telling every story rightly, or justice will not be fulfilled. And it *will* be fulfilled:

"Then you will look and be radiant,
   your heart will throb and swell with joy;
the wealth on the seas will be brought to you,
   to you the riches of the nations will come" (Isaiah 60:5).

Imagine—after your enemies are judged and banished, great treasure chests are then brought in and set before you. Huge oak chests; it requires two men or angels to bring each one in, and there are several. Jesus tells you to open them.

You ask, "What are these, Lord?" and he replies, *These are the gifts I meant for you in your former life but were stolen or prevented from making it to you. I return them now, with interest.* Imagine all that fills those chests. You hear laughter coming from one, for so much of what has been lost are memories and joy. I am weeping as I write this.

Then you turn to your right and ask, "And what are these chests, Lord?" *These are the rewards for your life's choices, your victories, your perseverance, and your service. In addition to your estates, of course,* he says with a smile.

Those treasure chests are yours, friends; their contents will thrill your heart and redeem so much of what you have endured here. Justice shall be yours, justice personal and particular. Wrongs will be avenged, hurts shall be healed, and all that was stolen from you in this life will be recompensed far beyond your wildest hopes. You will open those chests, look, and be radiant. Your heart will throb and swell with joy (pages 146–148).

» Have you considered that we have a role to play in the administration of justice when the evil one and all in his service are sentenced? What thoughts come to mind as you picture yourself with the Lord when this justice is carried out?

» What stirs the deepest emotion in you regarding the story of the treasure chests? Is it the realization that God knows all that has been lost or stolen from you and desires to return those things with interest? Or is it imagining what's inside your personal treasure chest? Be specific.

What Do We Actually *Do*?

Evil is gone. The world is restored. *We* are restored. Justice has been served, and we are lavishly rewarded. The only natural thing to do, the only appropriate thing to do at that point, is pop a cork, open a cask, push back the furniture, and throw a riotous party! Of course we all head off to celebrate at a feast; I have no doubt it carries on for weeks, probably months! There are quite a few stories that need telling, and many reunions that must take place.

Then what? What do we do *after* the wedding feast of the Lamb? Honestly, I think this is as far as most people have ever given it thought.

If we do talk at all about the joy of the coming kingdom, we talk about the feast, and nothing more. Our imaginations seem to end right there, falling off the edges of the banquet like ancient sailors feared they would fall off the end of the world. I am looking forward to the gala, for sure, but at some point the feast comes to a close, and just as every newly married couple drives away from their reception, we then have the rest of our unending life before us. What do we *do* with it?

This is probably the one aspect of our future most shrouded in religious vapors, fogged in by a pea soup of vagueness, emptiness, and heavenly foam—what is it that we *do* (pages 151–152)?

» Most feasts rarely last more than a few hours. Yet I picture the Wedding Feast of the Lamb as a "riotous party," lasting for weeks or perhaps months. How does that change your perception of this gathering? What are some of the sights, sounds, and smells that you imagine will fill this celebration?

» Are you curious what you will do in the New Earth after the Wedding Feast wraps up? Put words to some of your desires and longings, letting your imagination run wild.

The Excitement Has Only Just Begun

The next chapter of our story is precisely that—the chapter that *follows* all the chapters before and fits them perfectly. God is still telling a story; the next chapter is not disconnected from the rest. (I know it feels totally disconnected, but it is not.) If we will look at our future in light of the story God *has been* telling, it will banish the fog like a strong summer sun....

Our powerful and creative Father makes us in his image—powerful and creative sons and daughters. He gives us the earth like a wedding present, instructs us to reign, and endows each human being with talents and gifts to carry out that task. Father, Son, and Holy Spirit also included in the earth a latent potency—veiled powers and treasures, things like music and literature and science "hidden" in creation like Easter eggs so we might have the joy of discovering them. "Hey—look at this! I'm starting to put some things together, and I think it's called 'music.' There are notes and chords, meter, and if you stretch a string just right it makes a perfect C! Isn't this *incredible*?!"

Think of the potential that was waiting in the first Eden for glorious men and women to discover.

The long story of human history then follows, filled with glory and tragedy. God's children prove themselves capable of marvelous works; we also prove ourselves capable of terrible deeds. Evil ravages the earth and the human race. Things go from bad to worse until our loving Father intervenes; Jesus Christ comes to overthrow the evil one and ransom us. He begins the healing of our lives; he gives each of us a role in the church's great mission.

In the *next* chapter, our powerful and creative Father *re*-creates us and the earth. He then tells us to do exactly what he told Adam and Eve to do: *reign*. "You have made them to be a kingdom and priests to serve our God, and they will reign on the earth" (Revelation 5:10). Do you follow the story? Do you see the exciting connection? Glorious men and women are once again given a glorious world in order to do the very things it is in our nature to do. Only this time around with far greater powers, magnificent even. We have within *us* a latent potency, talents and gifts unrealized, soon to be made new; the renewed earth will be even more responsive to our leadership than the first time around (pages 154–156).

» This coming chapter of our story is precisely that—the chapter that *follows* all the chapters before and fits them perfectly. Have you viewed your life and the chapter when all things are made new as one continuous story God is telling? Why or why not?

» What will you do in the coming kingdom? The simple, stunning answer is, *you will do everything you were born to do.* How would you describe what that will be?

All Things New

At the epicenter of the renewal of all things is a *city*. And not just any city—it is the city of God, his very own home where he makes his dwelling with mankind (see Revelation 21:2-3, 9-16).

A massive, stunning, glorious place, whose presence allows us to think about the renewal of the arts and sciences, education, and the trades. The promise is that God will make not "some things new" but *all things new*.

Begin with the obvious—we know there is music in the kingdom. Just think of what the music will be! . . . Think of all the talented musicians who dwell there! We get to hear the work of the great composers, played by their own hand. We will hear the angels sing in their own tongues as well. . . . Follow me now—but who *makes* that music? Who makes the instruments upon which that music is played? You do, my friends. At least, those of you who want to will. . . .

I would love to learn other languages—and won't it be wonderful that every tribe and tongue is there to teach us? Speaking of learning, imagine the scope of education in the city! Jonathan Edwards believed that learning will be one of the great pleasures of the kingdom. He pointed out that though we are resurrected, we are still finite beings. I doubt very much that God would simply "dump" all knowledge into us the moment we arrive. We grow and develop in the kingdom by learning, with renewed and strengthened minds filled with the Holy Spirit. Imagine taking philosophy from Thomas Aquinas or any of the great thinkers from the ages; Pascal perhaps (though he might be busy teaching math). Saint Paul will hold classes on the Torah; Galileo will give lectures on the stars.

I expect we will study history under the very figures who lived in those eras. . . . Lincoln will teach classes on the Civil War, and Churchill will retell the Battle of Britain. I'm not quite sure how imagination and memory come together to honor history; perhaps we will "see it" as it is being told by those who lived it. Perhaps we will go further and *enter into it*—for all times are accessible to our glorious God, and he keeps all times within himself. There is no question those stories and episodes will be accessible to us somehow, and vividly (pages 157–160).

» What have you always dreamed of doing? What gifts have you yearned to express?

» How does it feel to know that you'll be able to experience this in the New Earth?

Think of the sciences in the kingdom! . . . What new glories are waiting to be discovered? Wonders leading to wonders leading to creative breakthroughs only imagined in science fiction on this side.

And what of the trades? We know we have homes and dwellings in the kingdom—who furnishes those homes? Who makes the chairs, the tables, the tapestries? I've always wanted to work with my hands. I would love to have the time and skill and mentors to build boats with hand tools and sail them, learning to navigate by the stars. Again, I am not being fanciful; I am utterly serious. You are healed and restored as a human being. . . . These things are part of your personhood; they are how God created you, and they will be even more glorious in the *re*-created you. Dream, my friends. . . .

Certainly storytelling is one of the great pleasures in the kingdom. God clearly takes it very seriously—he made reality in the shape of a story. Would you like to write? Illustrate? Act? Produce? Perhaps we get to take workshops from the great artists! These things are not obliterated when we step into the life to come; God renews *all* things. Dallas Willard assures us,

> We will not sit around looking at one another or at God for eternity but will join the eternal Logos, "reign with him," in the endlessly ongoing creative work of God. It is for this that we were each individually intended, as both kings and priests (Exodus 19:6; Revelation 5:10). . . . A place in God's creative order has been reserved for each one of us from before the beginnings of cosmic existence. His plan is for us to develop, as apprentices to Jesus, to the point where we can take our place in the ongoing creativity of the universe.[14]

> Just as Adam and Eve were commissioned to, only this time around on a higher level, with greater powers, creatively engaged in very real and tangible things. We know we eat in the city; surely the joy of eating doesn't end with the feast. Who grows the food? Who brings it to market? What chefs prepare it? It is unlike God to just "zap" these things into existence while we sit around doing nothing, bored to death. He creates us to create (pages 160–162).

» To help access the hidden dreams and capacities in your own soul, ask yourself this question: *What have I watched someone else doing and longed to do as beautifully as they can?* Write that down.

» What it will be like when you will experience the fullness of that desire in the kingdom? Explain.

Hitting Your Full Stride

We haven't yet seen anyone in their true glory. Including you.

Yes, Mozart did start writing symphonies as a child, and Picasso could draw before he could talk. But most human beings are profoundly thwarted in their "calling" here because of wounding, assault, envy, or circumstances that would never let them fly. For most human beings on this planet, work ranges from disappointing to oppressive. What does the kingdom offer those men who work the Indonesian sulfur mines or the tens of millions of modern slaves upon the earth? This is not what God intended. How many Mozarts are there right now, hidden in slums and huts across the globe?

All your creativity and gifting will be restored and then some when *you* are restored. All of that latent potency inside of you—so damaged here, marred, frustrated, never given the opportunity to grow and develop and express itself—all of it completely restored, including your personality. From there you are able to act in the new world in ways far greater than Adam and Eve were able to act the first time around (and look at what humanity has been able to do with "be fruitful . . . rule" [Genesis 1:28] in a broken world!). You will have absolute intimacy with Jesus Christ, and his life will flow through your gifts unhindered (pages 170–171).

» Not only will your gifting be fully restored in the New Earth, but
so will your personality. How do you think the transformation
of your personality might impact and upgrade your creativity?

» Imagine what you will be capable of; how vast your powers will
be in the New Earth! You know you shall walk on water, for Peter
did on this earth at Jesus' bidding. How far do you think your
creative and artistic capacities will reach?

What will you do in the life to come? Everything you were born
to do. Everything you've always wanted to do. Everything the kingdom *needs* you to do.

THE BIG IDEAS

» All of the great stories borrow their power from the one
true story.
» Evil will be fully and finally overthrown.
» We will reign with God and pursue our gifting in the
coming kingdom.

GROUP DISCUSSION

Watch the video for session 4. If you find it helpful, use the following space to take a few notes on anything that stood out to you.

Teaching Notes

Discussion Questions

After the teaching session has ended, discuss as a group any or all of the following questions.

1. Have you noticed how all great stories and epic movies follow the same storyline? All is good in the kingdom, evil enters into the story, a rescuer comes, and a great battle ensues where evil is overthrown and the kingdom is restored to its glory. What are several books or movies where you see these themes at play? How are they borrowing their power from our story?

2. **Read Revelation 19:1–2.** You have a heart for redemption and for justice to be rightly served. Think about a specific evil that has plagued members of your family, friends, or community over time. What evil are you most looking forward to finally being vanquished?

3. **Read Revelation 20:10.** What will it be like when the familiar temptations and struggles you've faced are no longer issues— not due to your successful resistance, but because the enemy no longer exists?

4. In the video, I ask you to imagine a scene where there are huge treasure chests. Some hold things from your former life that were stolen by the enemy—such as your joy or cherished memories. Other chests contain rewards for your service and perseverance. What do you hope will be in your treasure chests?

5. Have you considered how God, from the beginning, has filled this earth with hidden treasures—like music, science, and literature—so you might have the joy of discovering them with him? What talents and gifts has God given you to pursue? How might those interestd be even more fully realized in the New Earth?

6. **Read Revelation 5:9–10.** We will reign one day as restored human beings on a restored earth. What do you sense that may involve or look like?

7. What are you looking forward to learning in the kingdom? Perhaps mastering a new language or an instrument? Or maybe surfing or sculpting? How about learning history from the very people who lived it? Let your imagination run wild here.

GROUP EXERCISE

When all things are made new, we will be completely restored with all our creative powers, gifting, and calling in ways that were never fully realized in this life. Share with everyone what, for you personally, that might look like. Dream big.

THE POWER OF OUR HOPE

One of the most stunning recorded moments in all history took place as Jesus of Nazareth was dying on those Roman timbers. To his right and left hung criminals, sentenced and executed for actual crimes. . . . Bitterness had already seized one convict. . . .

But a light was about to break into darkness for the other: "Jesus, remember me when you come into your kingdom." Jesus answered him, "Truly I tell you, today you will be with me in paradise" (Luke 23:42–43).

Have any more startling, more assuring words ever been spoken? Immensity cloistered in one dear sentence. Today. Before the sun goes down. I'm staggered by the certainty of Jesus. . . .

Remember—this is a man being tortured unto death. Yet he speaks such rock-solid promise. He must *know* it to be true.

—JOHN ELDREDGE, *All Things New*

PERSONAL PREPARATION

This week, read chapters 9 and 10 in *All Things New:* "The Marriage of Heaven and Earth" and "Grab Hold with Both Hands." Begin with your reaction to these chapters. What did this arouse in you?

The Marriage of Heaven and Earth

We should talk about heaven for a moment because the New Earth changes our perspective and our thoughts about our future. I want to say as clearly as I can—nothing I have written here is intended to diminish the beauty, hope, or truthfulness of heaven. Heaven is where your dear loved ones who died in Christ are now. . . . Should you or I die before the *palingenesia*, we will immediately be in that paradise ourselves, thank the living God. Jesus is currently in heaven too, along with our Father, the Holy Spirit, and the angels. Which makes it a breathtaking place!

> But you have come to Mount Zion, to the city of the living God, the heavenly Jerusalem. You have come to thousands upon thousands of angels in joyful assembly, to the church of the firstborn, whose names are written in heaven. You have come to God, the Judge of all, to the spirits of the righteous made perfect, to Jesus the mediator of a new covenant, and to the sprinkled blood that speaks a better word than the blood of Abel (Hebrews 12:22–24).

Heaven is absolutely real and precious far beyond words. It is the "rest of" the kingdom of God, the "paradise" Jesus referred to. The city of God is currently there.

For the time being.

Remember—Peter explained in his sermon that Jesus remains in heaven *until* his return, when all things are made new:

> "Heaven must receive him until the time comes for God to restore everything, as he promised long ago through his holy prophets" (Acts 3:21).

Until—so much gravity and excitement contained in that word, such patient anticipation. When the time comes for God to restore everything, Jesus *leaves* heaven and comes to earth. To stay. The heavenly Jerusalem comes to earth, and "God's dwelling place is . . . among the people" (Revelation 21:3). Heaven is not the *eternal* dwelling place of the people of God. The New Rarth is, just as Revelation says. Just as the entire promise of the renewal of all things says. Just as Jesus explained, and the Bible declares.

Better said, we get heaven *and* earth; both realms of God's great kingdom come together at the renewal of all things. Then will we truly say, "It's heaven on earth." For it will be.

Jesus is in heaven at this moment, but Jesus is anxiously awaiting another Day. He is readying his armies; he is cinching the straps on his saddle. There is another event his attention is absolutely fixed upon: "the Son of Man coming in his kingdom" (Matthew 16:28) (*All Things New*, pages 173–175).

» "Heaven is not the *eternal* dwelling place of the people of God." How has your understanding of heaven and the New Earth changed during this study?

» One day we really will get heaven on earth. What great event acts as the catalyst for heaven and earth coming together at the renewal of all things (see Matthew 16:28)?

That Great and Fateful Day

Whenever the church is wrestling to understand or recover some treasure of the faith, it is always a good idea to return to what Jesus himself had to say about the matter. After all, this is his story. It is his teaching on the *palingenesia* that set us out on our wondrous journey here. Where exactly does Jesus want us to fix our future hopes?

"Again, it will be like a man going on a journey, who called his servants and entrusted his wealth to them. . . . After a long time the master of those servants returned and settled accounts with them" (Matthew 25:14, 19).

He said: "A man of noble birth went to a distant country to have himself appointed king and then to return" (Luke 19:12).

"Therefore keep watch, because you do not know on what day your Lord will come" (Matthew 24:42).

"Be dressed ready for service and keep your lamps burning, like servants waiting for their master to return from a wedding banquet" (Luke 12:35–36).

Jesus clearly wanted us to interpret the story from the vantage point of his *return*.

Heaven is very, very precious. Heaven is the paradise of God. But if you will notice—I say this reverently, carefully—heaven is not the great anticipated event the writers of the New Testament look forward to.

And we are eagerly waiting for him to return (Philippians 3:20 NLT).

. . . as you eagerly wait for our Lord Jesus Christ to be revealed (1 Corinthians 1:7).

. . . looking for and hastening the coming of the day of God (2 Peter 3:12 NKJV).

Therefore, with minds that are alert and fully sober, set your hope on the grace to be brought to you when Jesus Christ is revealed at his coming (1 Peter 1:13) (pages 175–177).

» According to Scripture, where exactly does Jesus want us to fix our future hopes?

» Heaven wasn't the main event the writers of the New Testament were anticipating. Why do you think so many Christians today talk more about heaven than the return of Jesus?

The great hope and expectation of the Christian faith is focused on one dramatic, startling event, sudden as a bolt of lightning, sharp as the tip of a sword: the bodily return of

Jesus Christ, and with that, the renewal of all things. The two are united, as surely as God the Father and God the Son are united—the renewal of all things awaits the coming of our Lord, and the coming of our Lord ushers in the renewal of all things. . . .

The historic church held the return of Christ to be so central to the Christian faith that they felt it could not be put aside or buried as some peripheral doctrine without losing Christianity itself. C. S. Lewis wrote,

> There are many reasons why the modern Christian and even the modern theologian may hesitate to give to the doctrine of Christ's Second Coming that emphasis which was usually laid on it by our ancestors. Yet it seems to me impossible to retain in any recognizable form our belief in the Divinity of Christ and the truth of the Christian revelation while abandoning, or even persistently neglecting, the promised, and threatened, Return. "He shall come again to judge the quick and the dead," says the Apostles' Creed. "This same Jesus," said the angels in Acts, "shall so come in like manner as ye have seen him go into heaven." "Hereafter," said our Lord himself (by those words inviting crucifixion), "shall ye see the Son of Man . . . coming in the clouds of heaven." If this is not an integral part of the faith once given to the saints, I do not know what is[15] (pages 177–178).

» Have you considered how inseparable the bodily return of Jesus and the renewal of all things are to each other? Which one have you focused on more? Why do you think that is?

» Which part of the C. S. Lewis quote on Christ's Second Coming resonates most with you? Explain why.

But When?

Now, yes, yes—I know great damage has been done by those who ignore the words of Christ that we cannot predict his coming and go on to predict his coming. Announcements were made, and the world mocked us as the predicted Day passed without so much as a tremor. But from that fact it does not follow that you should therefore not think about it at all. Throughout Scripture we are urged to look for the return of Jesus, watch for it, wait for it eagerly. And yes—it does seem that given it has been two thousand years, it could be quite a few more. But it could *also* be tonight. Our Lord and God spoke very stern warnings about a particular attitude toward his return:

> "Who then is the faithful and wise servant, whom the master has put in charge of the servants in his household to give them their food at the proper time? It will be good for that servant whose master finds him doing so when he returns. Truly I tell you, he will put him in charge of all his possessions. But suppose that servant is wicked and says to himself, 'My master is staying away a long time,' and he then begins to beat his fellow servants and to eat and drink with drunkards. The master of that servant will come on a day when he does not expect him and at an hour he is not aware of. He will cut him to pieces and assign him a place with the hypocrites, where there will be weeping and gnashing of teeth" (Matthew 24:45–51).

First, did you notice the reward again? The master puts the faithful servant in charge of *all his possessions*! He does not destroy the farm and take his servant somewhere else; he gives his servant the whole estate, the heavens and earth. But did you also notice the forbidden attitude: "my master is staying away a long time"?

Pause and let that sink in—he's "staying away a long time" is called the "wicked" attitude. It is the *forbidden* attitude. And the one most of you probably have embraced.

> "Be dressed ready for service and keep your lamps burning, like servants waiting for their master to return from a wedding banquet, so that when he comes and knocks they can immediately open the door for him. It will be good for those servants whose master finds them watching when he comes. Truly I tell you, he will dress himself to serve, will have them recline at the table and will come and wait on them. It will be good for those servants whose master finds them ready, even if he comes in the middle of the night or toward daybreak. But understand this: If the owner of the house had known at what hour the thief was coming, he would not have let his house be broken into. You also must be ready, because the Son of Man will come at an hour when you do not expect him" (Luke 12:35–40).

We are urged to watch and be ready. Your watchfulness is further commanded with the warning that he will return at exactly the hour when everyone thinks he's still a long ways off. Like this hour right now, or any one close to it. . . .

Where is this supposed coming? The current expression of that goes much more cleverly, like this: "But *every* age has thought that Jesus was about to show up. Even Paul did—and he was wrong. Who knows when it could be; it might take another thousand years." It sounds so reasonable . . . except for the fact that this is the forbidden attitude. Yes, every age has thought that Christ would return any moment, and well they should. They were right to do so because "any moment" could have been their moment. They were right to have expected his return because they were commanded to by Christ himself. They were wise to do so because it is the *antidote* to so many harmful things; when the "wicked servant" embraces the posture that his master is still far off, he turns his heart toward the indulgences of this world, trying to slake his kingdom thirst with everything within reach (pages 178–181).

» Can you recall a past prediction about the return of Christ? Describe it—as well as the effect it had on your heart in terms of whether you are now more expectant or hesitant to discuss his Second Coming.

» What is the forbidden attitude, and why it is so dangerous for believers? Have you ever embraced this attitude? Explain.

This Changes a Lot of Things

Jesus *will* return. Swiftly, unexpectedly. Any moment. His return will usher in the renewal of all things. That includes the execution of justice, rewards, the feast, your "estates," your appointed role in his great kingdom—along with the restoration of everything you love. This has some pretty staggering implications.

For one thing, it ought to radically transform our attitude toward death.

Losing someone you love is an earthquake; it is traumatic. Because what we *see* is the death, what we *experience* is the massive sudden and ongoing loss, death is filled with tragedy and mockery. It seems to have the last word, whatever our creeds may say. We do not yet see the resurrection; we do not yet see the renewal of all things, and so we are vulnerable to massive agreements with loss and devastation, even with grief. But the moment we allow life to win, the moment we accept Jesus' "I'm just going away for a bit," it changes everything. . . .

But far too often Christians experience the death of a loved one as devastation. We even feel it is appropriate to be devastated and make massive agreements with it. By feeling utterly heartbroken we feel we are honoring the ones we have lost. . . .

I am not making light of grief nor loss. I am very familiar with them. But we must, we must keep before us the reality that our dear ones are not dead at all. They are more alive now than they have ever been. . . .

Let me push it a step further. Jesus and the saints down through time actually *longed* for the day they left this vale of tears and stepped into Life itself. As Paul confided, "I desire to depart and be with Christ, which is better by far" (Philippians 1:23). Better by far—is that our attitude toward our own passing? . . .

So the desperate grasping at life you see in our world, the drastic measures when someone is well along in years, the grasp at any and every form of treatment—these should not be practiced by Christians. It makes no sense at all. Why the desperate clinging to buy yourself or a loved one a year or two more? We have lost perspective. We have forever; we have the world made new, forever (pages 183–185, 187).

» Why should the coming return of Jesus radically transform our attitude toward death?

» Jesus and the saints actually "longed for the day they left this vale of tears and stepped into Life itself." How would our fear of death lose its sting and power to intimidate if we embraced this mindset?

The True and Only Heaven

You have a heart for the kingdom of God; your longing for Life is the essential part of you. And that precious heart must only be given to the kingdom of God, not the counterfeits so abundant in the world today. Which brings us back to shepherding our hope—and the hopes of others. Never before has the world been more in need of an unbreakable, brilliant, and tangible hope.

For the renewal of all things has a very, very sober reality to it:

I saw the Holy City, the new Jerusalem, coming down out of heaven from God, prepared as a bride beautifully dressed for her husband. And I heard a loud voice from the throne saying, "Look! God's dwelling place is now among the people, and he will dwell with them. They will be his people, and God himself will be with them and be their God. 'He will wipe every tear from their eyes. There will be no more death' or mourning or crying or pain, for the old order of things has passed away."

He who was seated on the throne said, "I am making everything new!" Then he said, "Write this down, for these words are trustworthy and true."

He said to me: "It is done. I am the Alpha and the Omega, the Beginning and the End. To the thirsty I will give water without cost from the spring of the water of life. Those who are victorious will inherit all this, and I will be their God and they will be my children. But the cowardly, the unbelieving, the vile, the murderers, the sexually immoral, those who practice magic arts, the idolaters and all liars—they will be consigned to the fiery lake of burning sulfur. This is the second death" (Revelation 21:2–8).

A shudder just ran down my spine.

Evangelism has really slipped into the background in our day, for very obvious reasons. In this climate of hatred, set in a worldwide culture of tolerance as the last remaining virtue, even the faintest suggestion that someone's opinions about faith and God might be incorrect triggers a violent reaction. The early Christians were not martyred because they believed in Jesus Christ; they were martyred because they would not *also* bow to Caesar as a god. They went to their deaths because their views were seen to be exclusivist—and indeed, they were. "Salvation is found in no one else, for there is no other name [but Jesus] under heaven given to mankind by which we must be saved" (Acts 4:12). This is the faith "once delivered"; this is your faith if you are a Christian. A very difficult line to walk at this moment.

God will make sure that everyone who wants to be there will be there. But our faith is not some soft pabulum of universal "whatever-ism." Justice cannot be justice if God were to simply ignore those who persist in hating him till the end. Hard as it is to believe, there are many who do not *want* to be a part of God's kingdom:

> "A man of noble birth went to a distant country to have himself appointed king and then to return. So he called ten of his servants and gave them ten minas. 'Put this money to work,' he said, 'until I come back.'
> "But his subjects hated him and sent a delegation after him to say, 'We don't want this man to be our king'" (Luke 19:12–14).

Startling. Inconceivable. But not everyone wants the joys of heaven-on-earth for the simple reason that they do not want Jesus to be king. His presence fills the kingdom: "The city does not need the sun or the moon to shine on it, for the glory of God gives it light" (Revelation 21:23). If you do not enjoy the highly filtered experience of his presence available now, what will you do when it is before you in fullness of glory (pages 189–191)?

» Read Revelation 21:2–8 again. What are your thoughts about this very sober reality to the renewal of all things?

» "In a worldwide culture of tolerance as the last remaining virtue, even the faintest suggestion that someone's opinions about faith and God might be incorrect triggers a violent reaction." Have you ever experienced this type of reaction when sharing the exclusive message of Jesus with others? Explain.

Grab Hold with Both Hands

I have been told that now . . . I am supposed to "make it all practical."

Several well-intentioned counselors have urged me to finish by turning our focus to making a difference in the world today. It struck me as a hard right turn in a fast-moving train, but I've been warned that millennials especially want to talk about justice now, not heaven later. I understand the advice; I have empathy for where it comes from. But if I were you—it was spoken regarding you, dear reader—I would find it as offensive as a racial smear. As if your heart were so little and your mind so incredibly narrow you cannot possibly value the treasure of hope. As if you believe the pain of the world is due to the fact that people just have way too much hope right now.

The constant push in Western Christianity to "make it practical" betrays our favorite apostasy—it exposes how utterly fixated on the present moment we really are.

Yes, we need to embody God's love in the world today. The human race is not well; things fall apart. We must care for the planet and all creation; we must fight injustice. But we speak of that work so casually; we do not understand it can be the most demanding, heartbreaking work in the world. . . . "If you read history," wrote C. S. Lewis, "you will find that the Christians who did most for the present world were precisely those who thought most of the next. It is since Christians have largely ceased to think of the other world that they have become so ineffective in this."[16]

If you really want to make a difference in the world, the best thing you can do is exactly what the Scriptures command you to do—grab the promised Renewal with both hands and make it the anchor of your soul:

> We who have run for our very lives to God have every
> reason to grab the promised hope with both hands

and never let go. It's an unbreakable spiritual lifeline, reaching past all appearances right to the very presence of God (Hebrews 6:18–19 MSG). . . .

If you woke each morning and your heart leapt with hope, knowing that the renewal of all things was just around the corner—might even come today—you would be one happy person. If you knew in every fiber of your being that nothing is lost, that everything will be restored to you and then some, you would be armored against discouragement and despair. If your heart's imagination were filled with rich expectations of all the goodness coming to you, your confidence would be contagious; you would be unstoppable, revolutionary. . . .

Oh yes, we need to make this practical. We need to take this hope so seriously we sell everything to buy this field. We must make this utterly real and tangible, so that over time our souls are truly anchored by it (pages 197–201).

» The push to make Western Christianity practical reveals how utterly fixated we are on this present moment. What are some ways this preoccupation with the present can sabotage our hope in the coming kingdom?

» C. S. Lewis makes the powerful observation that "it is since Christians have largely ceased to think of the other world that they have become so ineffective in this." Why do you think this is true?

Giving Our Hearts to the Kingdom

Here is a good beginning—what are the first three things you plan to do when you enter the kingdom?

I'm serious. . . . What are the first three things you plan to do? Where are the first three places you want to visit? Is there some special spot . . . from your childhood that you would love to return to? The sound of the rain on a tin roof as you fell asleep at night? The smell of orange sticky buns fresh from the oven on Christmas morning? Remember—it is the child-heart in you that is far readier to embrace the kingdom. This isn't wishful thinking; this isn't "How enchanting!" Either you believe the kingdom is coming, or you do not. If you do believe, now you understand that the kingdom means the restoration of all things: "Look, I am making everything new!" (Revelation 21:5 NLT).

Given the suffocating, pathological unbelief and anti-romanticism of our post-postmodern culture, you are going to have to make very conscious choices to take hold of this hope. Allowance—*the renewal of all things might be true*—is not taking hold. Acceptance—*okay, I think it is*—is not taking hold. We need to grab this hope like we would hug the person in front of us if we were passengers on a wild motorcycle ride; we need to "take hold" like you do the top of a ladder when you suddenly think you are falling. *Seize* is a far better description; we need to *seize* this hope (pages 201–202).

» One way to begin to seize this hope with a good, firm grip is to ask yourself, *What have I done with my kingdom heart? Where am I currently taking it?* You have a heart for joy. Where is your hope for joy set right now?

» You ache for restoration, yours and those you love. Where is your hope for restoration these days?

» What are the first three things you plan to do at the renewal of all things? Begin making lists. Allow yourself to dream big. Do this for the simple reason that if this is not something you are making plans for, then your hopes are not really set there.

Filling the Treasury of Your Imagination

The dreams I began having about the kingdom only started this year. I have friends who seem to "see into" the kingdom, but I have never been that guy. I do hear from God; his words to me are precious beyond telling. But I've never been one to receive "pictures" or visions, let alone dreams. Then one day it struck me: *Maybe the reason I don't get pictures from God is because I don't ask for them.* "You do not have because you do not ask" (James 4:2). So I began asking.

And God began answering. Not only in dreams, but in all sorts of ways (he is eager to fill our hearts with hope!).

The sunrise out my window has become a regular reminder for me; I've come to look for the promise there every morning. I keep running into images of the kingdom in photos I see, so I've started to cut pictures out of magazines; I want to build a scrapbook of images of the New Earth. In fact, I spent several hours online last week looking through one of those stock photo websites, looking for images that had the special magic for me of the Great Renewal.

Movies are also filled with pictures of the Restoration. Stasi and I were watching *Tangled*—the Disney story of a princess stolen by an evil woman and held captive for decades. Every year her father and mother—the king and queen—release lanterns into the sky to commemorate her birthday and to proclaim the hope she will return one day. Far off in her prison tower, the captive princess sees those lanterns and something in her heart knows they are for her. Finally, she breaks free of the witch and makes it back to the city in time to see those lanterns for herself. A silly moment for the kingdom to break through, but I found myself quietly weeping for the day I get to come home to my Father-King, and the reception he will have for me.

You will be greatly helped by filling the treasury of your imagination with images of the coming Renewal; without them, it will be nigh impossible to make this the anchor of your soul. If you would take hold of this hope with both hands and never let go, you need to know what it is you are taking hold of.... The foggy and vague do not inspire, ever. As Peter Kreeft says, "It doesn't matter whether it's a dull lie or a dull truth. Dullness, not doubt, is the strongest enemy of faith."[17]

Ask Jesus to show you his kingdom.

Sanctify your imagination to him, all your spiritual gifting, and ask him to reveal to you pictures of the coming kingdom. Be specific—if you want to see the city, ask to see the city. If you want to see those waterfalls, ask to see them. You will need to be open to being surprised; do not "script" what you think you "should" see....

Stay open to surprises; keep asking for glimpses of the kingdom any way God wants to bring them. This is how we reach into the future to take hold of the hope that is our anchor. The more our imaginations seize upon the reality, the more we will have confident expectation of all the goodness coming to us.

And if you want to take a really big risk, for an even more beautiful and encouraging picture, ask Jesus to show you as he sees you, as you are in his kingdom. That one might take a little waiting for, because we are so fearful, but wait for it. It will be worth it (pages 206–208).

» What movies have you seen recently that seem to reflect images of the Restoration?

» Perhaps one reason we don't get pictures or images of the kingdom from God is because we don't ask for them. Have you recently asked Jesus to show you his kingdom? If so, what have you seen? If you never have, would you like to ask for them now?

The renewal of all things is the most beautiful, hopeful, glorious promise ever made in any story, religion, philosophy, or fairy tale. And it is *real*. And it is *yours*.

THE BIG IDEAS

» The return of Jesus—not heaven—is the great anticipated event of Scripture.
» The *forbidden attitude* is the belief that Jesus will not return for a long time.
» When we understand that nothing is lost, death loses its power to intimidate us.
» We live expectantly by giving our hearts and hopes fully to the kingdom.

GROUP DISCUSSION

Watch the video for session 5. If you find it helpful, use the following space to take a few notes on anything that stood out to you.

Teaching Notes

Discussion Questions

After the teaching session has ended, discuss as a group any or all of the following questions.

1. How often do you find yourself praying for the return of Jesus? If this hasn't been a regular part of your prayers, do you sense the practice might help shepherd your hopes for what is to come?

2. **Read Matthew 24:42; 25:14–19; Luke 12:35–36; and 19:12.** Given the emphasis of these passages, why do you think believers tend to focus on heaven more than the return of Jesus?

3. **Read Matthew 24:45–51.** What is the forbidden attitude in this parable? Is this attitude something you struggle with? Explain.

4. When it comes to death, we often grieve as if we'll never see our loved ones again. How would this change if we viewed their absence as temporary rather than permanent—knowing we'll be reunited with everyone we love who died in Christ?

5. **Read Romans 8:18–21.** In these current hard times, is your "joyful anticipation" deepening? What might you do for this to increase?

6. We need to fill our hearts with brilliant pictures and hopeful expectations of the coming kingdom. Imagine you have a magazine in front of you now. What pictures would you want to cut out and place in your journal as reminders of what is to come? Be specific.

7. As we come to the end of this study, where have your views of heaven, earth, and the restoration of everyting you love changed the most? Has there been a corresponding increase of hope with this new insight? Explain.

GROUP EXERCISE

At the end of this session, I revealed the first three things I want to do upon entering the kingdom. Now it's your turn. What are the first three things you hope to do? Why are those things specifically at the top of your list? Consider sharing this with the group.

LEADER'S GUIDE

Thank you for your willingness to lead your group through *All Things New: Heaven, Earth, and the Restoration of Everything You Love.* The rewards of leading are different from the rewards of participating, and we hope you find your own walk with Jesus deepened by this experience. This leader's guide will give you some tips on how to prepare for your time together and facilitate a meaningful experience for your group members.

What Does It Take to Lead This Study?

Get together and watch God show up. Seriously, that's the basics of how a small group works. Gather several people together who have a hunger for God, want to learn more about what is in store for them at "the renewal of all things" (Matthew 19:28), and are willing to be open and honest with God and themselves. The Lord will honor this every time and show up in the group. You don't have to be a pastor, priest, theologian, or counselor to lead a group through this study. Just invite people over, watch the video, and talk about it. All you need is a willing heart, a little courage, and God will do the rest. Really.

How This Study Works

There are three important pieces to the *All Things New* small-group study: (1) the book *All Things New,* (2) the five-session video study, and (3) this study guide. Make sure everyone in your group has a copy of the book and a study guide. It works best if you can get books and guides to your group *before* the first meeting. That way, everyone can read the first two chapters ahead of time and be prepared to watch the first video session together.

This series is presented in five video sessions, with each session approximately fifteen minutes in length. Each week, you'll meet together to watch the video and discuss the session. This series can also be used in classroom settings, such as Sunday school classes, though you may need to modify the discussion time depending on the size of the class.

Basically, each week you and your group will: (1) read the corresponding chapters in *All Things New*, (2) answer a few pre-session questions found in this guide, (3) watch one of the video sessions together, and (4) talk about it. That's it!

A Few Tips for Leading a Group

The setting really matters. If you can meet in a living room rather than a conference room in a church, do it. Pick an environment that's conducive to people relaxing and getting real. Remember the enemy likes to distract us when it comes to seeking God, so do what you can to remove these obstacles from your group (silence cell phones, limit background noise, no texting). Set the chairs or couches in a circle to prevent having a "classroom" feel.

Have some refreshments! Coffee and water will do; cookies and snacks are even better. People tend to be nervous when they join a new group, so if you can give them something to hold onto (like a warm mug of coffee), they will relax a lot more. It's human nature.

Good equipment is important. Meet where you can watch the video sessions on a screen that is big enough for everyone to see and enjoy. Get or borrow the best gear you can. Also, be sure to test your media equipment ahead of time to make sure that everything is in working condition. This way, if something isn't working, you can fix it or make other arrangements before the meeting begins. (You'll be amazed at how the enemy will try to mess things up for you!)

Be honest. Remember that your honesty will set the tone for your time together. Be willing to answer questions personally, as this will set the pace for the length of your group members' responses and will make others more comfortable in sharing.

Stick to the schedule. Strive to begin and end at the same time each week. The people in your group are busy, and if they can trust you to be a good steward of their time, they will be more willing to come back each week. Of course, you'll want to be open to the work God is doing in the group as members process these teachings about heaven and the New Earth. During such times, you may want to linger in prayer or discussion. Remember the clock serves *you;* your group doesn't serve the clock. But work to respect the group's time, especially when it comes to limiting the discussion times.

Don't be afraid of silence or emotion. Welcome awkward moments. The material presented during this study will likely challenge the group members to reconsider some of their long-held beliefs about the restoration of the earth. The idea that *nothing is ever truly lost* may evoke some emotions in them as they think back on their hardships and the losses they have experienced. Don't be afraid to ease into the material with the group.

Don't dominate the conversation. Even though you are the leader, you are also a member of this small group. So don't steamroll over others in an attempt to lead—and don't let anyone else in the group do so either.

Prepare for your meeting. Watch the video for the meeting ahead of time. Though it may feel a bit like cheating because you'll know what's coming, you'll be better prepared for what the session might stir in the hearts of your group members. Also review the material in this guide and be sure to spend time in prayer. In fact, the *most important* thing you can do is simply pray ahead of time each week:

> *Lord Jesus, come and rule this time. Let your Spirit fill this place.*
> *Bring your kingdom here. Take us right to the things we really*
> *need to talk about and rescue us from every distraction. Show us*
> *the heart of the Father. Meet each person here. Give us your grace*
> *and love for one another. In your name I pray.*

Make sure your group members are prepared. Before the first meeting, secure enough copies of the study guide and the *All Things New* book for each member. Have these ready and on hand for the first meeting, or make sure the participants have purchased these resources for themselves. Send out a reminder email or a text a couple of days before the meeting to make sure folks don't forget about it.

As You Gather

You will find the following counsel to be especially helpful when you meet for the first time as a group. I offer these comments in the spirit of "here is what I would do if I were leading a group through this study."

First, as the group gathers, start your time with introductions if people don't know one another. Begin with yourself and share your name, how long you've been a follower of Christ, if you have a spouse and/or children, and what you most want to learn about heaven, the New Earth, and the restoration of everything you love. Going first will put the group more at ease.

After each person has introduced himself or herself, share—in no more than five minutes—what your hopes are for the group. Then jump right into watching the video session, as this will help get things started on a strong note. In the following weeks you will then want to start by allowing folks to catch up a little—say, fifteen minutes or so—with some "hey, so how are you?" kind of banter. Too much of this burns up your meeting time, but you have to allow some room for it because it helps build relationships among the group members.

Note that each group will have its own personality and dynamics. Typically, people will hold back the first week or two until they feel the group is "safe." Then they will begin to share. Again, don't let it throw you if your group seems a bit awkward at first. Of course, some people *never* want to talk, so you'll need to coax them out as time goes on. But let it go the first week.

Insight for Discussion

If the group members are in any way open to talking about their lives as it relates to this material, you will *not* have enough time for every question suggested in this study guide. That's okay! Pick the questions ahead of time that you know you want to cover, just in case you end up only having time to discuss a few of them.

You set the tone for the group. Your honesty and vulnerability during discussion times will tell them what they can share. How *long* you talk will give them an example of how long they should. So give some thought to what stories or insights from your own work in the study guide you want to highlight.

WARNING: The greatest temptation for most small group leaders is to add to the video teaching with a little "teaching session" of their own. This is unhelpful for three reasons:

1. The discussion time will be the richest time during your meeting. The video sessions have been intentionally kept short so you can have plenty of time for discussion. If you add to the teaching, you sacrifice this precious time.

2. You don't want your group members to be *teaching, lecturing,* or *correcting* one another. Every person is at a different place in his or her spiritual journey. If you use a lecturing or correcting tone, the group will feel like they have the freedom to teach one another. That can be disastrous for group dynamics.

3. The participants will have read the corresponding chapters in *All Things New,* done the preparation work in this guide, and watched the video teaching. They don't need more content! They want a chance to talk and process their own lives in light of all they have taken in.

A Strong Close

Some of the best learning times will take place after the group time as God brings new insights to the participants during the week. Encourage group members to write down any questions they have as they read through *All Things New* and do the preparation work. Make sure they know you are available for them as they explore what God has to say about the restoration of the earth, as many of the concepts might be new or challenging to them. Finally, make sure you close your time by praying together. Perhaps ask two or three people to pray, inviting God to fill your group and lead each person during this study.

Thank you again for taking the time to lead your group. May God reward your efforts and dedication and make your time together in *All Things New* fruitful for his kingdom.

ENDNOTES

1. "Outlandish Proverbs", ed. George Herbert, in *The Complete Works in Verse and Prose of George Herbert*, vol. 3 (1640; repr., London: Robson and Sons, 1874), 324.

2. G. K. Chesterton, *Orthodoxy* (1908; repr., Chicago: Moody Classics, 2009), 20–22.

3. Ibid., 82.

4. Nick Jans, *A Wolf Called Romeo* (Boston: Houghton, Mifflin Harcourt, 2014).

5. C. S. Lewis, *God in the Dock* (Grand Rapids: Eerdmans, 1970), 87, emphasis mine.

6. C. S. Lewis, *The Last Battle* (New York: HarperCollins, 2002), 213–214, 219.

7. C. S. Lewis, *The Silver Chair* (New York: HarperCollins, 1953), 237–239.

8. Gary Black, *Preparing for Heaven* (New York: HarperOne, 2015), 29.

9. Richard Louv, *Last Child in the Woods* (Chapel Hill, NC: Algonquin Books, 2005), overall theme of the book.

10. J. R. R. Tolkien, *The Lord of the Rings* (1954; repr., New York: Houghton Mifflin Harcourt, 2004), 952–953.

11. Thomas Cahill, *How the Irish Saved Civilization* (New York: Random House, 1995), 117–118.

12. C. S. Lewis, *The Weight of Glory* (New York: Touchstone, 1975), 26.

13. "Prostitution Statistics," Havocscope: Global Black Market Information, http://www.havocscope.com/prostitution-statistics.

14. Dallas Willard, *The Divine Conspiracy* (San Francisco: HarperCollins, 1998), 378.

15. C. S. Lewis, *The World's Last Night and Other Essays* (New York: Harcourt, 1952), 93.

16. C. S. Lewis, *Mere Christianity* (1952; New York: HarperOne, 1980), 135.

17. Peter Kreeft, *Everything You Ever Wanted to Know About Heaven* (San Francisco: Ignatius Press, 1990), 20.

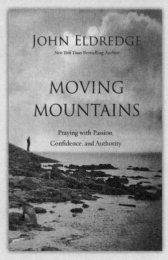
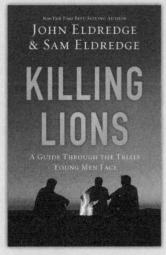

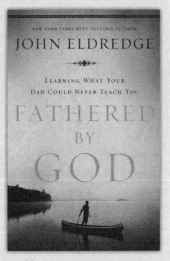

MORE RESOURCES FROM
RANSOMED HEART

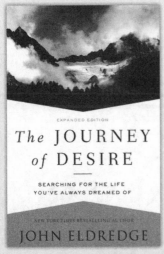

STUDY GUIDE AVAILABLE

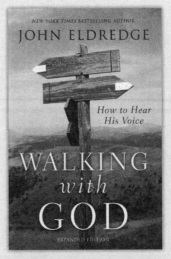

VIDEO CURRICULUM AND
STUDY GUIDE AVAILABLE

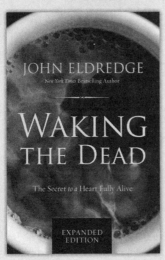

STUDY GUIDE AVAILABLE

VIDEO CURRICULUM AND
STUDY GUIDE AVAILABLE

FOR MORE PROJECTS AND INFORMATION
VISIT US AT **RANSOMEDHEART.COM**